Inglés Marítimo

Ana López Pampín - Iria González Liaño

www.netbiblo.com

IUEM
Instituto Universitario
de Estudios Marítimos
www.udc.es/iuem

> **Ficha de catalogación bibliográfica**
>
> Inglés Marítimo
> • 1ª Edición
> Ana López Pampín - Iria González Liaño
> NETBIBLO, S.L., A Coruña, 2004
> ISBN: 84-9745-059-0
> Materia: Transportes Fluviales y Marítimos 656
> Formato: 17 x 24 cm. • Páginas: 192

INGLÉS MARÍTIMO

No está permitida la reproducción total o parcial de este libro, ni su tratamiento informático, ni la transmisión de ninguna forma o por cualquier medio, ya sea electrónico, mecánico, por fotocopia, por registro u otros métodos, sin el permiso previo y por escrito de los titulares del Copyright.

DERECHOS RESERVADOS 2004, respecto a la primera edición en español, por
  © Instituto Universitario de Estudios Marítimos

ISBN: 84-9745-059-0
Depósito Legal: C-2004-2004
Editor: Carlos Iglesias
Maquetación: PDG, S.L.
Impreso en: JosmanPress
Impreso en España - Printed in Spain.

CONTENIDO

Prólogo 5

1 El puerto 7
    Introducción 9
    1. Tipologías portuarias 9
    2. Áreas portuarias 11
    3. Infraestructura portuaria 14
    4. Servicios portuarios 15
    5. Personal portuario 18
    6. Tarifas portuarias 18

2 El buque 21
    Introducción 23
    1. Partes del buque 23
    2. Tripulación 26
    3. Tipos de mercancía 28
    4. Tipos de contenedores 29
    5. Tipos de buques 30

3 Los agentes del transporte marítimo 35
    Introducción 37
    1. Agentes marítimos 37
    2. Organismos 38

4 Contratos de transporte marítimo 41
    Introducción 43
    1. *Charter Party* (Póliza de Fletamento) 43
        1.1. Clasificación 47
    2. *Bill of Landing* (Conocimiento de Embarque) 69
    3. Contrato de remolque 77
    4. Contrato de salvamento 86

5 Incoterms-Cláusulas de transporte 89
    Introducción 91
    1. Los Incoterms 91

6	**Las comunicaciones**	101
	Introducción	103
	1. Expresiones propias de la comunicación marítima	105
	2. *Message markers*	106
	3. Identificadores de emergencia...	108
7	**La meteorología**	111
	Introducción	113
	1. Escala Beaufort..	113
	2. Escala Douglas	114
	3. Mareas...	114
8	*Maritime transport glossary*	117
	1. English-Spanish	119
9	**Glosario de transporte marítimo**	139
	1. Español-Inglés..	141
10	**Siglas de transporte marítimo**	159
	Bibliografía	169
	Las señales marítimas internacionales de banderas *International maritime signal flags*	175
	Galería de imágenes	183

PRÓLOGO

El nuevo contexto de la globalización se caracteriza por la mayor intensidad de los flujos comerciales, por la movilidad de los capitales, por las menores trabas y obstáculos al comercio y por una mayor uniformización de las relaciones económicas internacionales. Esta intensa armonización internacional constituye uno de los principales pilares que caracterizan los procesos de internacionalización de la economía.

Pero estas connotaciones inherentes a las cuestiones económicas no constituyen el único y excluyente *leitmotiv* que guía y ampara todos los razonamientos que enmarcan las dinámicas de la globalización.

Visualizamos, asimismo, distintas normas que van asociadas a los agentes y a los operadores; observamos diferentes fórmulas organizativas y empresariales vinculadas a las peculiaridades específicas de cada territorio; y destacamos la intensa velocidad, intensidad y alcance que adquiere la circulación de ideas y de decisiones que permiten una propagación muy particular y global a la vez, en perfecta coexistencia y asimétrica rivalidad. Este juego de elementos es lo que una vez sedimentado constituye nuestro *savoir-faire*; que se puede proceder a trasmitir como un *know-how* acumulado hacia otras latitudes y espacios.

En el marco del Master de Administración Marítima y Gestión Portuaria que desarrolla el Instituto Universitario de Estudios Marítimos de la Universidade da Coruña los alumnos reclamaban, con toda la razón del mundo que, a la vista de que el lenguaje se está convirtiendo en un input imprescindible para homologar cualquier grado y nivel de cualificación profesional; y que constituye, a la vez, un rasgo esencial para adecuarnos a las normas que imperan en el funcionamiento de las actividades marítimas, era imprescindible contar con material adecuado y de apoyo, actualizado y centrado en el quehacer cotidiano que sirviera para incrementar nuestro valor y para acumular más factores diferenciales a nuestro favor.

Conscientes de nuestras obligaciones nace la oportunidad de disponer de un material (output) que ofrezca dichos conocimientos en lo tocante a las cuestiones referidas a los puertos, a las mercancías, a los mecanismos operativos y a los formularios básicos; a la vez que integre aquellas cuestiones que se refieran al funcionamiento de los operadores, agentes y gestores de las actividades marítimas.

Acometer tal tarea no fue fácil al existir otros materiales, por cierto muy útiles, en otras Universidades y centros de formación internacionales. Nuestro interés radicaba en ofertar un texto muy práctico, muy útil, muy manejable y muy rápido. Por eso, encargamos la confección de un texto de Inglés Marítimo a personas que han estado con nosotros familiarizándose con la terminología, con la operativa portuaria y marítima, y con la enseñanza. Esto es, quisimos que las personas encargadas de tal misión poseyeran la experiencia necesaria para abordar el cometido que se les encargaba y al mismo tiempo que pudieran abordarlo con éxito.

El resultado final, a mi juicio, es sumamente válido. Varios rasgos así lo avalan. En primer lugar, se ha utilizado un lenguaje que se centra, exclusivamente, en aquellos elementos claves, eliminando lo superfluo. En segundo lugar, se caracteriza por la concreción, evitando cualquier grandilocuencia y elementos accesorios. Y en tercer lugar, destaca porque se centra en lo esencial e imprescindible, excluyendo lo no-necesario.

La definición del contenido del trabajo ha sido, pues, un acierto como lo fue la elección de las autoras. Las dos personas que han realizado el libro combinaron las necesidades que planteaban los alumnos del Master (familiaridad con la terminología y vocación docente) con la reclamación profesional (exigencia y rigor en el contenido), interpretando perfectamente ambas demandas. La combinación de una licenciada en Filología Inglesa con una licenciada en Traducción e Interpretación supuso abarcar dichos requerimientos y poder ofertar un producto final que colma nuestras aspiraciones.

Un estupendo escritor gallego, ya fallecido, al prologar un libro llegó a afirmar que el autor poseía una "fuerte musculatura mental". Lo rubricaba para enaltecer la capacidad del responsable del texto y resaltar su fuerza. No quisiera rescatar este concepto para subrayar el excelente trabajo que presentamos, sino que lo traigo a colación para añadir que las autoras, Ana e Iria, son jóvenes licenciadas por las Universidades de Galicia, poseedoras de auténtica vocación por la enseñanza, con fuerte compromiso social y con altas dosis de responsabilidad por su trabajo. Estas tres notas no son fáciles de encontrar en las universidades europeas; puesto que es costumbre encontrar un cierto pasotismo, una conducta relajada y una ausencia de cumplimiento en los objetivos marcados.

Estamos, en suma, ante un libro del que las autoras son sinónimo de tenacidad por el trabajo bien hecho; de constancia y de conseguir hacer de manera excelente la tarea encomendada. Es además, un libro que uno prologa con mucha facilidad, porque puede asegurar que va a poseer una amplia aceptación, y porque sirve para mejorar conocimientos, ampliar saberes y constituye una base muy sólida para vehiculizar nuevas relaciones.

Con este objetivo y con la misión cumplida, el IUEM les emplaza a nuevos compromisos en próximas fechas.

Fernando González Laxe
Director del Instituto Universitario de Estudios Marítimos.

1
El puerto

Introducción

El puerto es el área urbana, natural o artificial, dispuesta para el atraque y desatraque de embarcaciones que ofrece la infraestructura y los servicios necesarios para desarrollar las diferentes actividades, tanto de carácter comercial, como lúdico o deportivo. Estratégicamente situados, generalmente en la franja costera o fluvial, los puertos permiten operaciones de carga, descarga, embarque, desembarque, almacenamiento, distribución, etc.

A lo largo de la historia, el concepto de puerto como simple receptor de embarcaciones ha ido evolucionando hasta llegar a convertirse en un enclave logístico, con fuertes intereses económicos, en los que se realizan importantes operaciones de tráfico portuario.

Un factor que ha influido de manera destacada en dicha evolución es la aparición del *transporte multimodal*, ya que los puertos han de ofrecer no sólo instalaciones para el desarrollo de las actividades marítimas, sino que también han de ser ejes de comunicación con otros medios de transporte: terrestres, aéreos, ferroviarios, etc.

Una definición ajustada al concepto de puerto en la actualidad sería la siguiente: El puerto es un interfaz que combina los distintos medios de transporte; es un área multifuncional, comercial e industrial en la que se realiza el manejo de la mercancía en tránsito para facilitar su distribución dentro de la cadena logística global, de origen a destino; se ha pasado del concepto de transporte "puerto-puerto" (*port to port*), al concepto de transporte "puerta-puerta" (*door to door*).

1. Tipologías portuarias

Pueden realizarse varias clasificaciones con respecto a los puertos, atendiendo a los siguientes criterios: funcional, geográfica, evolutiva, administrativa y logística,

a) Clasificación funcional. Según la función en que se especializa cada puerto.

Clasificación Funcional de Puertos	
Commercial Port	Puerto Comercial
Free Port	Puerto Libre
Industrial Port	Puerto Industrial
Military Port	Puerto Militar
Mixed Port	Puerto Mixto
Passenger Port	Puerto de Pasajeros
Refugee/Shelter Port	Puerto Refugio
Yatching Port	Puerto Deportivo
Fishing Port	Puerto Pesquero

b) Clasificación geográfica. Atendiendo a la ubicación del puerto, bien en la franja costera marítima, bien en las orillas de un río o un lago.

Clasificación Geográfica de Puertos	
Maritime Port	Puerto Marítimo
Fluvial Port	Puerto Fluvial
Lake Port	Puerto Lacustre

c) Clasificación evolutiva. De acuerdo con los cambios experimentados por los puertos con el paso del tiempo, se pueden distinguir tres tipos de puertos. Los puertos de primera generación son aquéllos construidos hasta los años 60, dedicados exclusivamente a tareas de carga, descarga y almacenamiento, aislados de la economía local. Los puertos de segunda generación, construidos entre los años 60-80, son puertos con una mayor dimensión económica, industrial y comercial. Por último, los puertos de tercera generación surgen en los años 80, convirtiéndose en plataformas logísticas que integran el transporte multimodal; aparece un nuevo concepto: el puerto seco, cuyo objetivo es ampliar el área de distribución comercial, en enclaves no costeros y con buenas comunicaciones. Según la definición de la UNCTAD (*United Nations Conference for Trade and Development*) el puerto seco "es una instalación no costera de uso publico, distinta de un puerto y de un aeropuerto, aprobada por un organismo competente, equipada con instalaciones fijas y ofreciendo servicios para manipular y almacenar temporalmente cualquier clase de mercancías incluyendo contenedores - que sea considerada como "en tránsito" para efectos de aduanas, por cualquier modo de transporte de superficie no costero, y que tiene además la capacidad de efectuar controles aduaneros que permitan a estas mercancías continuar su tránsito, terminar el viaje y ser utilizadas localmente, ser despachadas para exportación, o ser re-exportadas según sea el caso."

Clasificación Evolutiva de Puertos	
First Generation Port	Puerto de Primera Generación
Second Generation Port	Puerto de Segunda Generación
Third Generation Port	Puerto de Tercera Generación
Dry Port	Puerto Seco

d) Clasificación administrativa. Según el tipo de gestión, podemos hablar en primer lugar de Puerto Propietario, en el que la Autoridad Portuaria es dueña de las infraestructuras, otorgando concesiones a empresas privadas para que desarrollen servicios integrales, de remolque, practicaje, etc.; en este caso, los operadores portuarios o empresas portuarias se responsabilizan de la inversión y el mantenimiento de las infraestructuras. En el Puerto Instrumento la Autoridad Portuaria también es dueña de las infraestructuras, de la superestructura y equipamientos y cede parte de los servicios a empresas privadas. Finalmente, tenemos el Puerto Operador, o Puerto de Servicios, en el que la totalidad de las instalaciones son propiedad de la Autoridad Portuaria y los servicios y actividades son gestionados y prestados por empresas portuarias, responsables del mantenimiento de las instalaciones y equipamientos.

Clasificación Administrativa de Puertos	
Landlord Port	Puerto Propietario
Tool Port	Puerto Instrumento
Operating/Comprehensive Port	Puerto Operador/Exportador

e) Clasificación logística. El puerto eje está dedicado exclusivamente a las principales líneas regulares, que distribuyen y reciben mercancía de grandes buques para dirigirla hacia otros puertos de menor calado o capacidad, como pueden ser el puerto alimentador, el puerto de tránsito, o puertos menores nacionales.

Clasificación Logística de Puertos	
Hub Port	Puerto Eje
Feeder Port	Puerto Alimentador
Transhipment Port	Puerto de Tránsito
Domestic Port	Puerto Nacional/de servicios

2. Áreas portuarias

El área portuaria comprende tanto los espacios marítimos, como los terrestres, en los que se desarrollan las distintas actividades o servicios.

Dentro del espacio marítimo se encuentra el canal de acceso, que constituye la vía de entrada al puerto; la zona de fondeo, donde los buques esperan para atracar en el muelle y comenzar las operaciones; el pantalán, embarcadero avanzado en el mar para amarrar barcos de pequeño tonelaje; y, por último, la dársena de maniobras, donde las embarcaciones giran y enfilan para atracar y desatracar.

En cuanto a la superficie terrestre puede hacerse una división entre las zonas más próximas al muelle o lugar de atraque, y las distintas zonas en las que se divide la explanada portuaria: de almacenamiento (bodegas, tanques, silos), de entrega y recepción de la carga, de circulación y maniobras (vías de acceso para otros medios de transporte), y de apoyo (talleres, edificios administrativos, aparcamiento).

Maritime Area	Superficie Marítima
Anchorage area	Zona de fondeo
Access chanel	Canal de acceso
Turning basin/Dock	Dársena de maniobras
Jetty	Pantalán

Terrestrian Area	Superficie Terrestre
Breakwaters/Mole	Rompeolas
Dock/Pier/Quay	Muelle
Dry Dock	Dique seco
Floating/Pontoon Dock	Dique flotante
Fish Market	Lonja
Delivery areas	Zonas de entrega
Traffic and turning areas	Zonas de circulación y maniobra
Support area	Zonas de apoyo
Storage/Warehousing areas	Zonas de almacenamiento
Duty-free zone	Zona franca

La infraestructura de un puerto depende del volumen y del tipo de carga que mueve. Atendiendo a estos factores, los puertos pueden presentar en su área terrestre distintos tipos de terminales.

Las terminales son aquellos lugares del puerto especializados en un determinado tipo de carga, que cuentan con instalaciones, equipamiento, y recursos humanos adecuados para llevar a cabo las funciones de manejo de la mercancía.

En función de la carga, las terminales se pueden clasificar en:

All Weather Terminal	Terminal cubierta.
Bulk Terminal	Terminal de graneles/graneleras.
Chemical Terminal	Terminal de productos químicos.
Container Terminal	Terminal de contenedores.
Dedicated Terminal	Terminal especializada; terminal explotada exclusivamente por una o varias compañías navieras para su uso particular.
Lo-lo Terminal	Siglas de *Lift-on/Lift-of*. modalidad de carga y descarga de buques en forma vertical.
Multi-purpose Terminal	Terminal multi-función; para la manipulación de distintos tipos de unidades de carga.
Oil Terminal	Terminal de combustibles/petroleras.
Passenger Terminal	Terminal de pasajeros.
Ro-ro Terminal	Siglas de *Roll-on/Roll-of*. Modalidad horizontal de carga y descarga por la que la carga es introducida en buques con entradas laterales, mediante el acceso de vehículos rodados a través de la rampa hasta su lugar de estiba.

3. Infraestructura portuaria

El conjunto de elementos y servicios que conforma la infraestructura portuaria varía según las actividades desarrolladas en un puerto; no obstante, existen equipamientos comunes a todos los puertos, entre los que cabría citar los siguientes:

Conveyor Belt: Cinta transportadora.

Crane: Grúa.

Fender (dolphin): Defensa (protección de madera u otros materiales para prevenir daños en el casco del buque durante las operaciones de amarre y desamarre.)

Forklift truck: Carretilla transportadora de paletas.

Hopper: Tolva.

Lighthouse: Faro.

Loading bridge: Puente de carga.

Reach stackers: Vehículo con plataforma elevadora.

Silo: Silo.

Truck (carrier): Carretilla transportadora.

Warehouse: Almacén.

La grúa es un elemento a destacar en el conjunto de la infraestructura portuaria, por la diversidad de funciones que desempeña, y por su implicación en todas las etapas de manipulación de la carga, tanto a bordo del buque, como en el propio puerto. Las grúas realizan servicios de carga, descarga, estiba, desestiba, almacenamiento, etc.

Según la función o la carga que manipulen, podemos hablar de distintos tipos de grúa:

Cranes	**Grúas**
Container crane	Grúa para contenedores
Deck crane	Grúa de cubierta
Jenny winch	Grúa de brazo fijo
Frame/Gantry/Portal crane	Grúa pórtico
Floating crane	Grúa flotante
Quayside crane	Grúa de muelle

En el siguiente gráfico se pueden observar las distintas partes que componen una grúa:

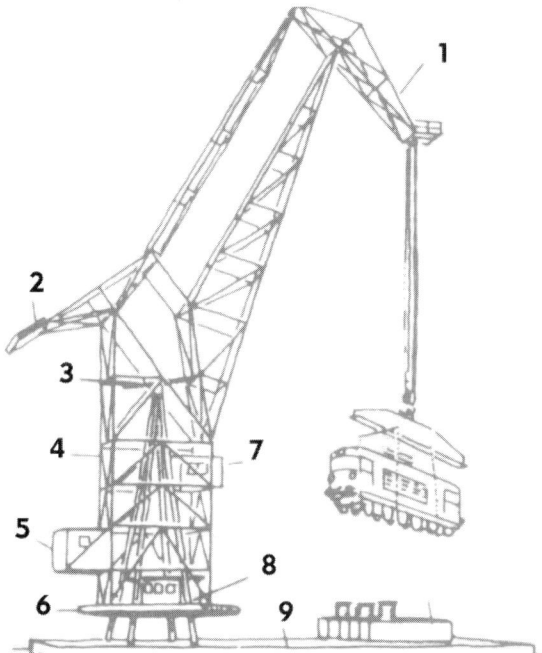

1. *Jib/Boom*: Brazo de la grúa.
2. *Counterweight/counterpoise*: Contrapeso.
3. *Adjusting spindle*: Eje ajustable.
4. *Crane framework*: Armazón de la grúa.
5. *Winch house*: Cabina del torno.
6. *Turntable*: Plataforma giratoria.
7. *Crane driver's cabin/cage*: Cabina del operario.
8. *Control platform*: Plataforma de control.
9. *Pontoon/Pram*: Pontón.

4. Servicios portuarios

En la siguiente figura se muestra la trayectoria de un buque desde su llegada a puerto hasta su salida, detallando las distintas operaciones a las que son sometidos tanto el buque como la carga.

En lo que concierne a dichas operaciones, consideramos conveniente aclarar los términos de *practicaje* y *estiba/desestiba*. El primero hace referencia a la asistencia técnica por parte del práctico del puerto al capitán para la conducción del buque hacia o desde el punto de amarre para su entrada o salida de puerto. Por su parte, la operación de *estiba* consiste en el traslado de la mercancía desde el momento en que es suspendida sobre la borda hasta que se sitúa en la cubierta del buque, mientras que en la *desestiba* se realiza el proceso inverso, trasladando la mercancía de la cubierta al muelle.

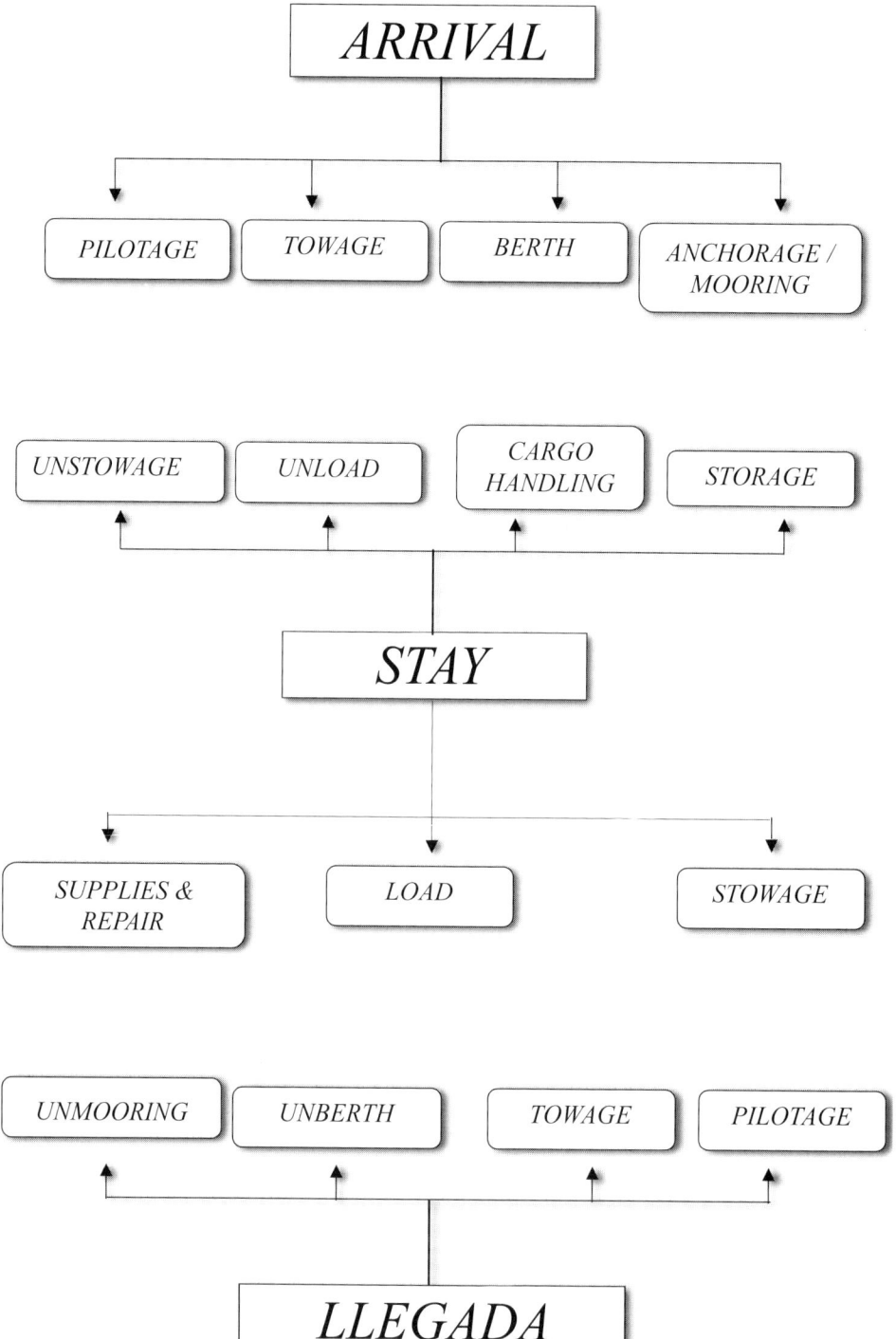

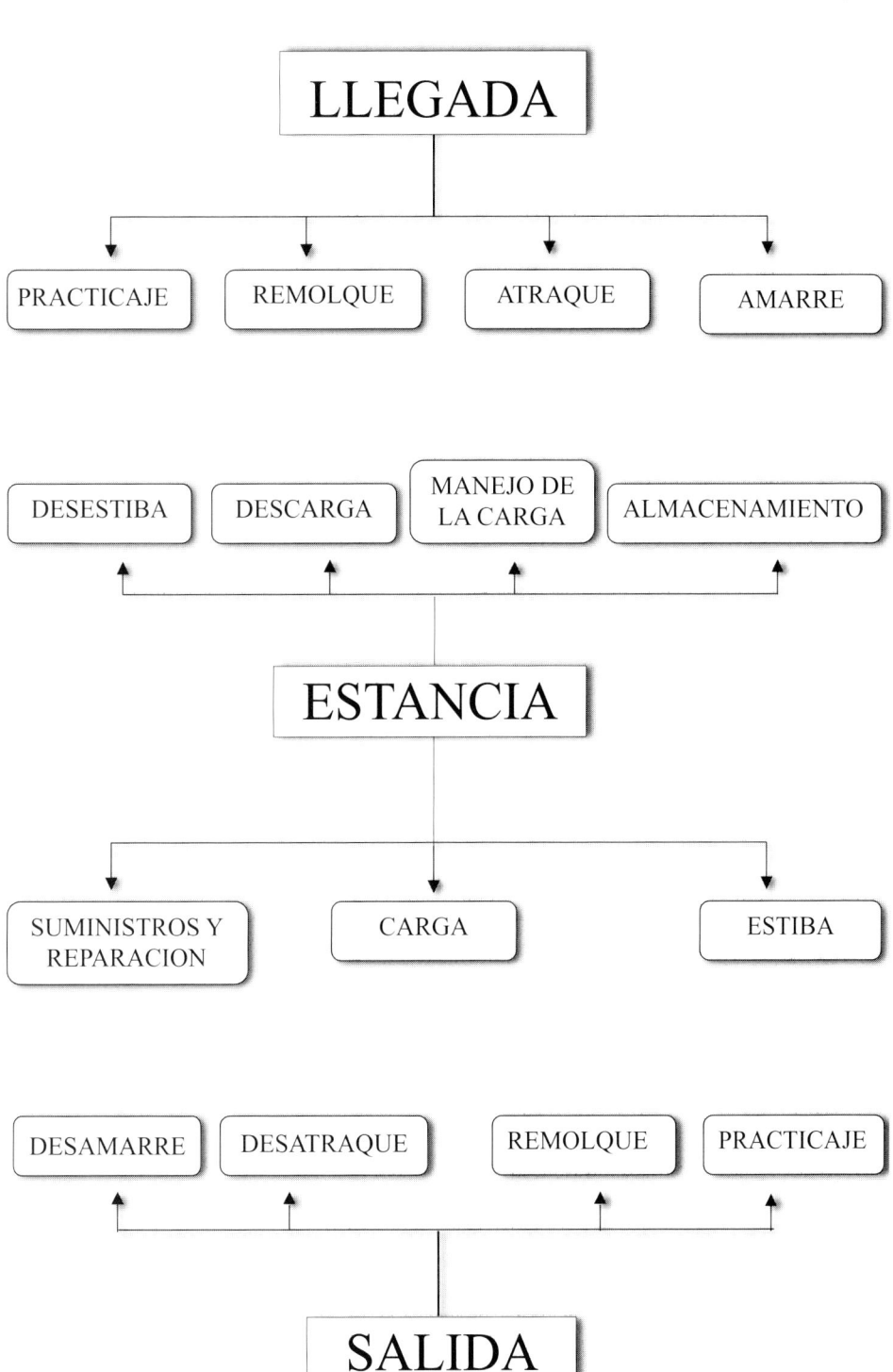

5. Personal portuario

Son varias las figuras que desempeñan las actividades portuarias para lograr que el puerto, como enclave comercial, sea eficiente.

PORT STAFF/PERSONAL PORTUARIO

- *Harbour Master*: Capitán del puerto.
- *Longshoreman*: Obrero portuario.
- *Shipbreaker*: Desguazador o chatarrero.
- *Shipbuilder*: Constructor de buques.
- *Stevedore*: Estibador.
- *Wharfinger*: Jefe de Muelle.
- *Shipping commissioner*: Comisario marítimo.
- Pilot: Práctico
  - *Inbound pilot*: Práctico de entrada.
  - *Outbound pilot*: Práctico de salida.

En el sistema anglosajón el práctico, sin pertenecer a la tripulación del buque, lo conduce en su llegada y salida a/de puerto; siendo momentáneamente empleado o dependiente del armador/naviero. Por el contrario, en el sistema latino, el práctico no conduce el barco, sólo asesora al capitán que sigue sus instrucciones

6. Tarifas portuarias

Al entrar en un puerto, los buques deben afrontar diferentes gastos en concepto de los servicios portuarios prestados:
- *Ship expenses*: Gastos del buque en puerto (provisiones, combustible, reparaciones …).
- *Port expenses*: Gastos de servicios al buque durante las maniobras de entrada y salida (practicaje, amarradores, tarifas …).
- *Handling expenses*: Gastos de manipulación de la mercancía (grúas, almacenaje …).

La suma de estos gastos se recoge en un solo documento llamado *Disbursement Account* (Cuenta de Escala), factura final de todos los servicios portuarios prestados al buque desde su entrada al puerto hasta el momento de salida.

Según la legislación española, se establece un cuadro de tarifas o tasas por la utilización de los servicios portuarios. Cada Autoridad Portuaria fija sus propias tarifas, sin que éstas sean inferiores al coste del servicio.

El pago de cada tarifa se corresponde con un servicio específico:

T-0: Utilización del sistema de ayudas a la navegación marítima, siendo de aplicación a todo buque que haga escala o se encuentre en las aguas de cualquier puerto nacional.

T-1: Acceso de los buques al puerto y su atraque o fondeo.

T-2: Acceso, embarque y desembarque de los pasajeros, y el uso de las instalaciones portuarias generales.

T-3: Uso de las instalaciones portuarias generales para la manipulación de la carga.

T-4: Acceso, atraque y fondeo de buques pesqueros, así como el uso de las instalaciones y servicios generales del puerto para los productos de la pesca.

T-5: Acceso, atraque y fondeo de las embarcaciones deportivas o de recreo, y el uso de las instalaciones generales portuarias por parte de sus tripulantes y pasajeros.

T-6: Utilización de grúas pórtico.

T-7: Uso de espacios, explanadas, y edificios para el almacenamiento de mercancías.

T-8: Uso de productos tales como agua, energía eléctrica, hielo, combustibles y otros productos entregados por la Autoridad Portuaria a los usuarios dentro de la zona portuaria.

T-9: Cualquier otro servicio prestado por la Autoridad Portuaria no incluido en los apartados anteriores.

	GENERAL TARIFFS	**TARIFAS GENERALES**
T-0	*Maritime signals*	Señales marítimas
T-1	*Vessel*	Buque
T-2	*Passengers*	Pasajeros
T-3	*Cargo*	Carga
T-4	*Fresh fishing*	Pesca fresca
T-5	*Sports and pleasure boats*	Embarcaciones de recreo

	SPECIFIC TARIFFS	**TARIFAS ESPECÍFICAS**
T-6	*Portal cranes*	Grúas pórtico
T-7	*Storages*	Almacenamiento
T-8	*Supplies*	Suministros
T-9	*Other services*	Servicios diversos

2
El buque

Introducción

El buque es el vehículo utilizado en el transporte marítimo, fluvial o en aguas interiores, que transporta mercancías o pasajeros, o realiza servicios marítimos, generalmente de ayuda a otras embarcaciones.

Es notable la evolución que ha experimentado este tipo de vehículos, desde los primeros barcos de vapor que realizaban cortos recorridos, pasando por la creación y utilización de buques transoceánicos, especializados en un determinado tipo de mercancías, primero a granel, más tarde pasajeros, hasta llegar a los buques portacontenedores, con una tendencia actual hacia buques de cada vez mayor tamaño.

El siguiente cuadro refleja, de manera somera, dicha evolución.

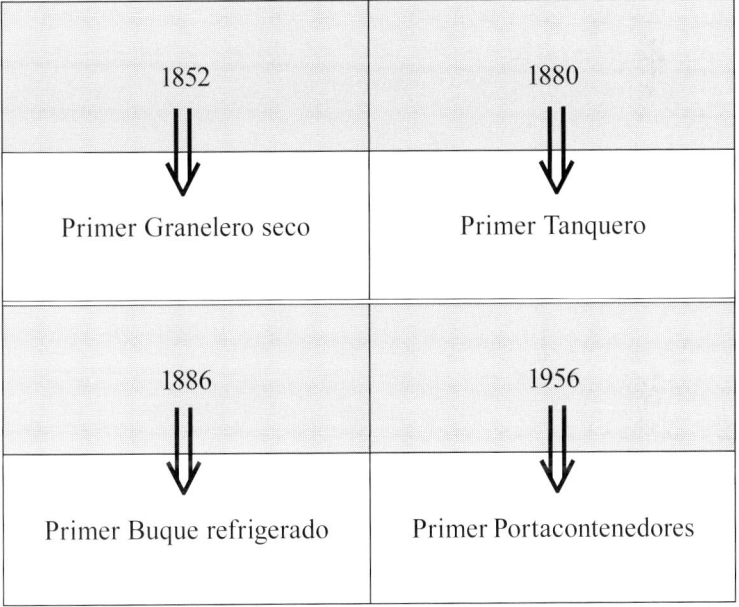

1. Partes del buque

Toda embarcación, independientemente de su tamaño o función, consta de casco y superestructura. El casco conforma el esqueleto de un barco, que comprende el espacio entre las bodegas y la cubierta superior y sirve de base para establecer las distintas posiciones a bordo. Por su parte, la superestructura incluye la sala de máquinas (zona de motores y calderas), y demás equipamiento de ayuda a la navegación (bombas, escotillas, equipo de fondeo y amarre, etc.).

En este apartado, a través de gráficos, se facilita la terminología relativa a los componentes de un buque, mostrando las distintas posiciones a bordo de un buque (Figura 1), las cubiertas (Figura 2), y, por último, los principales elementos que forman la estructura de un buque (Figura 3).

FIGURA 1. POSICIONES A BORDO DE UN BUQUE

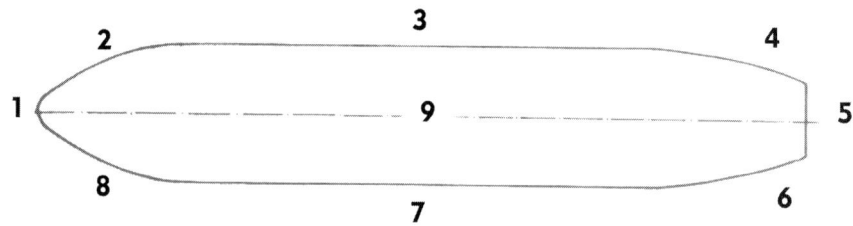

1. *Fore/bow*: Proa.
2. *Port bow:* Amura de babor.
3. *Port larboard*: Babor.
4. *Port quarter*: Aleta de babor.
5. *Aft*: Popa.
6. *Starboard quarter*: Aleta de estribor.
7. *Starboard*: Estribor.
8. *Starboard bow*: Amura de estribor.
9. *Amidship*: Crujía o medianía.

FIGURA 2. CUBIERTAS DE UN BUQUE

Las cubiertas de un buque se corresponden con los pisos de un edificio, dividiendo el casco en sentido horizontal y contribuyendo a dar forma a su estructura. El número y nombres de las cubiertas varía según el tipo de buque.

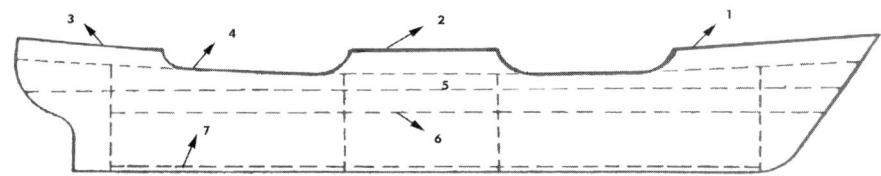

1. *Forecastle deck*: Cubierta de pasillo.
2. *Upper deck:* Cubierta superior.
3. *Poop deck:* Cubierta de toldilla.
4. *Weather deck*: Cubierta intemperie.
5. *Main deck*: Cubierta principal.
6. *Lower deck*: Cubierta inferior.
7. *Orlop deck*: Cubierta del sollado.

FIGURA 3. PARTES DEL BUQUE

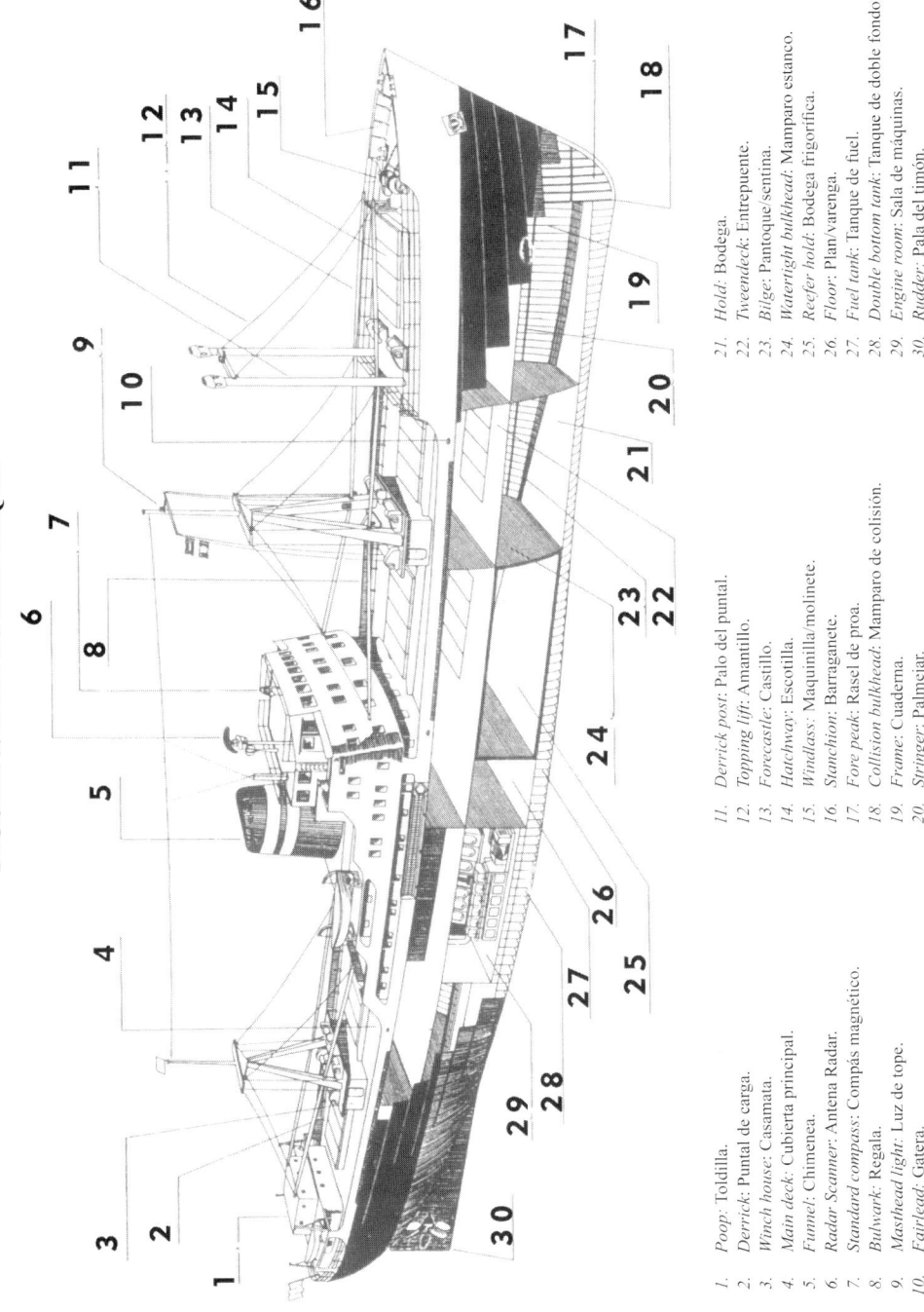

1. *Poop*: Toldilla.
2. *Derrick*: Puntal de carga.
3. *Winch house*: Casamata.
4. *Main deck*: Cubierta principal.
5. *Funnel*: Chimenea.
6. *Radar Scanner*: Antena Radar.
7. *Standard compass*: Compás magnético.
8. *Bulwark*: Regala.
9. *Masthead light*: Luz de tope.
10. *Fairlead*: Gatera.
11. *Derrick post*: Palo del puntal.
12. *Topping lift*: Amantillo.
13. *Forecastle*: Castillo.
14. *Hatchway*: Escotilla.
15. *Windlass*: Maquinilla/molinete.
16. *Stanchion*: Barraganete.
17. *Fore peak*: Rasel de proa.
18. *Collision bulkhead*: Mamparo de colisión.
19. *Frame*: Cuaderna.
20. *Stringer*: Palmejar.
21. *Hold*: Bodega.
22. *Tweendeck*: Entrepuente.
23. *Bilge*: Pantoque/sentina.
24. *Watertight bulkhead*: Mamparo estanco.
25. *Reefer hold*: Bodega frigorífica.
26. *Floor*: Plan/varenga.
27. *Fuel tank*: Tanque de fuel.
28. *Double bottom tank*: Tanque de doble fondo.
29. *Engine room*: Sala de máquinas.
30. *Rudder*: Pala del timón.

2. Tripulación

La tripulación en una embarcación, también denominada "dotación", está formada por toda persona contratada para desempeñar a bordo, durante un viaje, cometidos en relación con el funcionamiento o servicio de la nave, y que figura como tal en las listas de tripulación.

El sistema español incluye en este grupo no sólo a aquellos miembros que realizan funciones de marinería, sino también a los que desempeñan labores administrativas o técnicas. El número de personas que compone la dotación varía en virtud del tipo de embarcación.

Cada una de estas personas desempeña una función específica, destacando entre ellas el capitán (*Master*), primera figura a bordo, encargado de la dirección y gobierno para la conservación y salvación de tripulantes, pasajeros y mercancías; además de ser el representante del armador, que es quien lo designa. Históricamente la función del capitán era equivalente a la del armador en cuanto a toma de decisiones y gobierno, siendo a menudo copropietario del buque por lo que ejercía una doble labor, como profesional de la navegación y como comerciante. En la actualidad, debido a los avances tecnológicos, sus funciones son puramente técnicas y son otras figuras, como los consignatarios y demás agentes marítimos, los que actúan como representantes del armador en los distintos puertos.

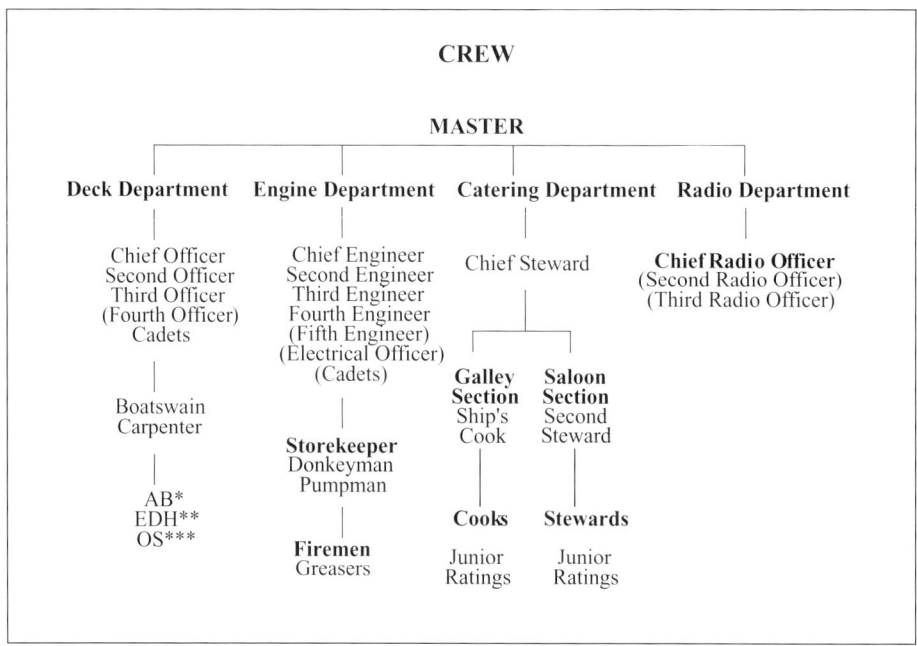

*   AB: *Able-bodied seaman*-Marinero capacitado.
** EDH: *Efficient Deck Hand*-Marinero de cubierta.
*** OS: *Ordinary Seaman*-Marinero.

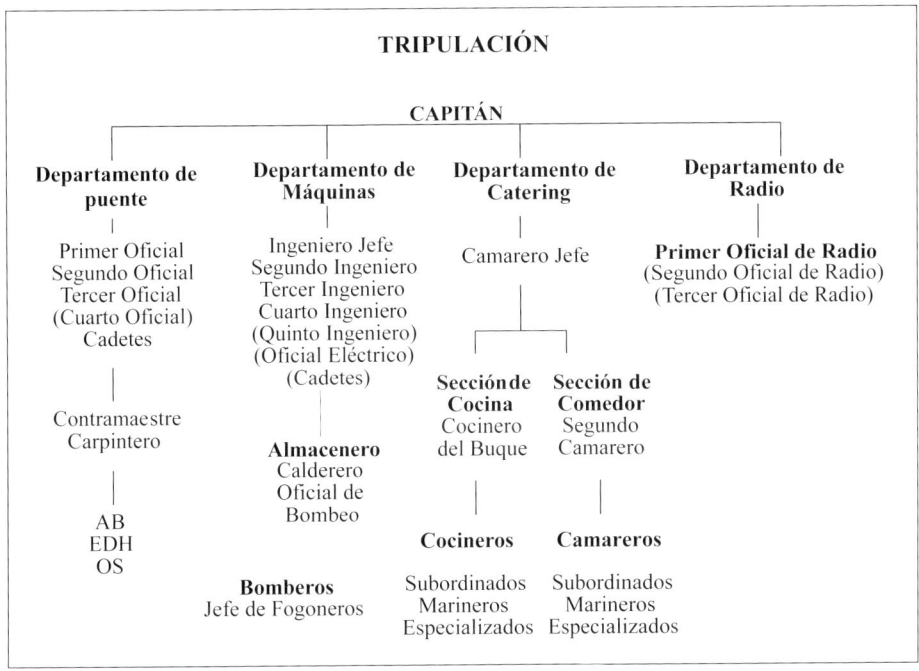

Tradicionalmente a bordo de un buque el tiempo se divide en periodos de cuatro horas, llamados *guardias (watches)*. Hay seis guardias, tal y como refleja el siguiente esquema:

00.00 - 04.00	Middle Watch
04.00 – 08.00	Morning Watch
08.00 – 12.00	Forenoon Watch
12.00 – 16.00	Afternoon Watch
16.00 – 20.00	Evening Watch
20.00 – 00.00	First Watch

La *Evening Watch* puede dividirse a su vez en dos guardias.

16:00 - 18:00 : *First Dog Watch*	Primer cuartillo
18:00 - 20:00 : *Second Dog Watch*	Segundo cuartillo

Distintos miembros de la tripulación se hacen cargo de las diferentes guardias.

	DECK	**ENGINE**
Middle Watch	Second Officer	Third Engineer
Morning Watch	Chief Officer	Second Engineer
Forenoon Watch	Third Officer	Fourth Engineer
Afternoon Watch	Second Officer	Third Engineer
Evening Watch	Chief Officer	Second Engineer
First Watch	Third Officer	Fourth Engineer

3. Tipos de mercancía

El concepto de mercancía abarca cualquier género vendible, objeto de trato o venta que puede transportarse con fines comerciales.

Los factores a tener en cuenta a la hora de clasificar la mercancía, en lo que respecta al transporte marítimo en particular, son la unidad de carga y las posibilidades de manejo de dicha mercancía.

La carga general es la carga que se mueve en paletas, plataformas que evitan que la carga se sitúe a ras del suelo en las bodegas, lo que facilita su apilamiento y traslado por medio de carretillas. Está carga está embalada en sacos, cajas, bidones, etc.

Por el contrario, la mercancía a granel se transporta sin envase o embalaje de ningún tipo. En este caso se establece una división entre graneles sólidos (cereales, carbón, fosfato y otros minerales) y graneles líquidos (hidrocarburos y demás productos químicos).

Una tercera modalidad de mercancía es la denominada refrigerada, que generalmente se presenta embalada, pudiéndose considerar mercancía general, pero que requiere unas condiciones atmosféricas determinadas por tratarse de mercancías perecederas que necesitan una temperatura concreta para su conservación, para lo que se requieren buques especializados.

Por último habría que hablar de la mercancía contenerizada. Este tipo de mercancía se transporta en cajas cerradas y selladas, los llamados contenedores, que pueden cargarse en cubierta o en la bodega del buque, y que facilitan el manejo y traslado de la mercancía. En el siguiente apartado se especifican los distintos tipos de mercancías.

General cargo	Carga general
Dry cargo	Carga seca
Liquid cargo	Carga líquida
Bulk cargo	Carga a granel
Reefer cargo	Carga refrigerada
Containerised cargo	Carga contenerizada

4. Tipos de contenedores

El contenedor ha supuesto una revolución en todas las modalidades de transporte. En un principio este tipo de embalaje era utilizado sólo en vías marítimas y por carretera, pero con el paso del tiempo se extendería al transporte ferroviario y aéreo.

El nacimiento del contenedor tiene lugar en 1956 cuando se decide utilizar cajas metálicas selladas para el transporte de mercancías, evitando así la manipulación y el posible deterioro de las cargas, y reduciendo el tiempo en el traspaso de la mercancía entre los distintos medios de transporte.

El organismo internacional ISO se ha encargado de estandarizar las medidas de los contenedores para facilitar las operaciones de traslado como pueden ser la estiba y desestiba. Las medidas más habituales de los contenedores son 20 y 40 pies, conocidos habitualmente por sus siglas inglesas: TEU (*Twenty Equivalent Unit*) y FEU (*Forty Equivalent Unit*). En cuanto a los materiales que se utilizan para su construcción, los más habituales son el acero, el aluminio (generalmente para contenedores frigoríficos), y la madera o fibra de vidrio, menos utilizados, ya que a pesar de su poco peso, no son materiales tan resistentes como el acero.

El transporte por medio de contenedores, en cualquiera de sus modalidades (marítimo, terrestre, aéreo o ferroviario), es una forma de transporte cada vez más en auge y que evoluciona con mucha rapidez. El motivo de esta rápida evolución es que la mercancía transportada de esta forma no se altere hasta su punto de destino; aunque también existen desventajas, ya que tanto las terminales portuarias como su infraestructura y equipamiento requieren una alta inversión.

Realizamos dos clasificaciones de contenedores; en primer lugar, atendiendo a su forma y, en segundo lugar, a las condiciones que reúnen con respecto a la mercancía que transportan.

Dentro de la primera clasificación, según su forma, hablamos de:

Standard/Dry van container	Contenedor standard. (Para mercancía de carga general)
Box container	Contenedor cerrado
Flat/Platform container	Contenedor plataforma
High cube container	Contenedor standard. (Gran capacidad)
Open side container	Contenedor de costado abierto
Open top container	Contenedor de techo abierto
Folding container	Contenedor plegable
Igloo container	Contenedor iglú

En la segunda categoría, según la mercancía transportada, los contenedores se clasifican en:

Bulk container	Contenedor granelero
Calorific container	Contenedor Isotermo (con sistema de calefacción)
Europallet container	Contenedor Europaleta (Estiba paralela con 2 paletas de medida europea)
Insulated container	Contenedor isotermo
Controlled Temperature container	Contenedor de temperatura controlada
Reefer/Con-air container	Contenedor frigorífico
Hanger container	Contenedor con colgadores para prendas de ropa
Tank container	Contenedor cisterna (cargas líquidas)

5. Tipos de buques

En cuanto a la clasificación de buques, existen cinco categorías básicas, respecto a la función que desempeñan: traslado de pasajeros, de pesca, buques de guerra, de carga, y buques auxiliares.

Los buques de pasajeros pueden ser de línea regular o cruceros, que realizan distintas rutas según la época del año. Por su parte, los denominados buques auxiliares se dedican a facilitar las maniobras de entrada o salida a puerto de otras embarcaciones, así como a socorrerlas en caso de accidente o situaciones de peligro para la navegación. Los buques de carga se clasifican en función de la carga que transportan, reuniendo las condiciones adecuadas para cada tipo de carga.

PASSENGER	**PASAJEROS**
Clipper ship	Navío rápido
Cruiser	Crucero
Excursion/Pleasure steamer	Vapor de recreo
Ferry	Ferry
Passenger liner	Trasatlántico

FISHING	PESCA
Fishing vessel	Buque pesquero
Trawler	Pesquero de arrastre

WAR	GUERRA
Aircraft carrier	Portaaviones
Battleship	Acorazado
Command ship	Buque de mando táctico
Destroyer	Destructor lanzamisiles
Frigate	Fragata
Landing craft	Buque de desembarco
Mine hunter	Cazador de minas
Minesweeper	Dragador de minas
Submarine	Submarino
Submarine chaser	Caza submarinos
Warship/Fighting ship	Buque de guerra

AUXILIARY SHIPS	BUQUES AUXILIARES
Barge/Lighter	Barcaza, gabarra
Bunkering boat	Lancha carbonera
Cableship	Cablero
Coaster ship	Barco de cabotaje
Dredger	Draga
Drilling vessel/Drillship	Perforadora
Fire-boat	Embarcación contra-incendios
Fire-fighting tug	Remolcador contra-incendios
Harbour ferryboat	Transbordador del puerto

AUXILIARY SHIPS	BUQUES AUXILIARES
Hooper	Ganguil
Hovercraft	Aerodeslizador
Ice breaker	Rompehielos
Jetfoil/Hydrofoil	Buque de propulsión a chorro
Lifeboat	Buque salvavidas
Lightship/Light vessel	Buque faro
Ocean tug	Remolcador de altura
Offshore tug	Remolcador para perforadoras
Pilot launch/Pilot boat	Lancha del práctico
Rescue cruiser	Buque de salvamento
Salvage tug	Remolcador de salvamento
Scow	Lanchón
Tender	Buque auxiliar
Tug/towboat	Remolcador

CARGO SHIPS	BUQUES DE CARGA
Barge carrier	Buque portabarcazas
Bulk carrier	Granelero
Coaler ship/Collier	Carbonero
Merchant ship	Buque mercante
Container ship/Container carrier	Buque portacontenedores
Tanker	Tanquero, buque cisterna
Crude carrier	Petrolero
Mothership	Buque madre, buque oceánico
Feeder	Buque alimentador

CARGO SHIPS	BUQUES DE CARGA
Freighter	Carguero
General cargo ship	Buque de carga general
Liner ship	Buque de línea regular
Tramp	Buque de tráfico irregular
Lo-lo ship (Lift-on/Lift-off)	Buque Lo-lo (carga y descarga vertical)
Ro-ro ship (Roll-on/Roll-off)	Buque Ro-ro (carga y descarga horizontal)

Con respecto a los denominados buques portacontenedores, el aumento de su tamaño es constante, debido a las mayores inversiones, los avances técnicos y el desarrollo de las líneas regulares, lo que trae consigo la reorganización del sistema de transporte y de la jerarquía portuaria. En la evolución del transporte marítimo, se habla de "cuatro revoluciones":

- La revolución *ship-to-shore*: utilización del contenedor en el transporte marítimo.
- La revolución *ship-to-rail*: aparición de la intermodalidad.
- La revolución *ship-to-ship*: surge el concepto de transbordo o *transhipment.*
- La "cuarta revolución": previsión de la llegada de buques de 15000 TEUs.

Esta evolución influye de manera importante en la transformación del buque portacontenedor; se pasa de los buques de Primera y Segunda Generación, con una capacidad de 2000 TEUs en la década de 1970; a los buques de Tercera y Cuarta Generación, surgidos en la década de 1980, en la que se establece un límite del tamaño de las embarcaciones debido a las restricciones dimensionales del Canal de Panamá; en ese momento a los buques de mayor tamaño, capacitados para cruzar el Canal de Panamá se les denominó Panamax. En 1989 entra en servicio el primer buque Post-Panamax, que supera las dimensiones de dicho canal. En el 2000 ya existen buques con capacidad para transportar hasta 8000 TEUs, y algunos expertos hablan de la construcción a largo plazo de buques de más de 15000 TEUs, los denominados Malacamax.

CONTAINERSHIPS	CONTENEDORES (TEU*)
Feeder	100-499
Feedermax	500-999
Handy	1000-1999
Subpanamax	2000-2999
Panamax	3000-3999
Post Panamax	>4000
New Panamax	12000
Malacamax	18000

*TEU: *Twenty Equivalent Unit.* Unidad equivalente a un contenedor de 20 pies.

3
Los agentes del transporte marítimo

Introducción

El transporte marítimo es una actividad comercial compleja en la que intervienen diferentes figuras, desempeñando cada una de ellas distintas funciones dentro de las etapas que conforman el transporte de mercancías.

1. Agentes marítimos

Un primer grupo está formado por aquellas figuras cuya actividad se centra en la explotación comercial del buque:

- El *shipowner* es el propietario del buque, naviero o armador, encargado de la explotación del buque, tanto náutica como comercial. Aunque el término en inglés es el mismo para ambos, existe una clara diferencia en español entre "armador" y "naviero". El naviero es el propietario del buque, que se encarga de explotarlo por su cuenta y riesgo y lo representa en el puerto en que se encuentre. Por su parte, el armador no tiene porque ser necesariamente el propietario del buque.

- El *carrier* es el transportista o fletante que se encarga de la explotación náutica de un buque, proporcionando al fletador un medio para el transporte de mercancías.

- El *charterer* es el fletador o agente de fletamento, es decir la persona física o jurídica que contrata un buque al transportista con fines comerciales, por un viaje o tiempo determinado, por lo que paga un flete.

En ocasiones, estas tres figuras actúan a través de agentes, delegando sus funciones por un tiempo y para una actividad determinada. Estos agentes trabajan como intermediarios, siempre en nombre del principal por el que han sido designados en un puerto en particular, a cambio de un porcentaje sobre el negocio pactado. Pueden desempeñar labores administrativas, técnicas y comerciales en un puerto concreto con respecto a la mercancía (carga, descarga, recepción y entrega) y al buque (suministros, reparación, etc.).

Cabe destacar los principales agentes:

- *Consignor*: Consignatario emisor, en representación del naviero, vinculado a éste por contrato de mandato y comisión mercantil. Puede actuar en nombre de varios principales o navieros. Sus obligaciones frente al naviero son de carácter administrativo, técnico y comercial: búsqueda de mercancía como comisionista (captación de cargas), atención al buque durante la escala, gestión de documentos ante la Autoridad Portuaria, Aduana, policía, capitanía marítima, etc.

- *Consignee*: Consignatario destinatario de las mercancías.

- *Forwarding agent*: Agente encargado de la tramitación del despacho aduanero que actúa en representación del transportista, en caso de importación o exportación de mercancías.

- *Freight forwarder*: Transitario. Operador intermediario que representa los intereses de los propietarios de la mercancía (importador o exportador), no del armador. Negocia con el armador o con sus agentes las condiciones de transporte de las mercancías desde su lugar de origen a su lugar de destino, organizando el transporte de la carga "door to door". No realiza los transportes materialmente, sino que los coordina, contrata y controla las operaciones.

- *Insurance broker*: Corredor de seguros. Encargado de la contratación del seguro del buque o de la carga. Esta función generalmente es asumida por el transitario.

- *Shipbroker*: Corredor marítimo. Persona física o jurídica totalmente independiente y gran conocedor de las líneas de un determinado puerto, cuyas funciones son la consulta o asesoramiento sobre la conveniencia o no de un contrato, estableciendo las relaciones entre su cliente y las otras partes interesadas. Pone en contacto a dos partes, fletador y fletante, actuando de intermediario entre exportadores e importadores y realizando las acciones necesarias para obtener una carga y gestionar su transporte. Trabaja a comisión o por una remuneración pactada y carece de responsabilidad en la ejecución de los contratos sobre los que asesora y negocia.

2. Organismos

Para llevar a cabo las actividades vinculadas al transporte marítimo, los agentes están sometidos a normativas que regulan aspectos como la seguridad marítima, la inspección técnica, y los controles de exportación e importación. Por ello, es necesario nombrar los siguientes organismos:

- *Ship Insurance Company*: Compañía aseguradora marítima. Empresa de seguros, cuya función es asegurar los distintos elementos que forman parte de una operación de transporte marítimo (carga, buque, responsabilidad civil).

- *Customs House*: Aduanas, servicio estatal encargado de la vigilancia y fiscalización de la exportación e importación de mercancías en el tráfico internacional.

- *Classification Society*: Sociedad de clasificación. Sociedad privada contratada por el armador del buque, cuya función consiste en realizar inspecciones técnicas con la finalidad de otorgar una certificación de seguridad de la embarcación.

- *P&I Club* (*Protection and Indemnization Club*): Club P&I (Club de Protección e Indemnización) Mutua aseguradora, formada por navieros y armadores, con la finalidad de asegurarse recíprocamente frente a posibles pérdidas derivadas de la actividad marítima.

Todo este engranaje del transporte marítimo de mercancías, y los agentes que en él intervienen, queda reflejado en el siguiente gráfico:

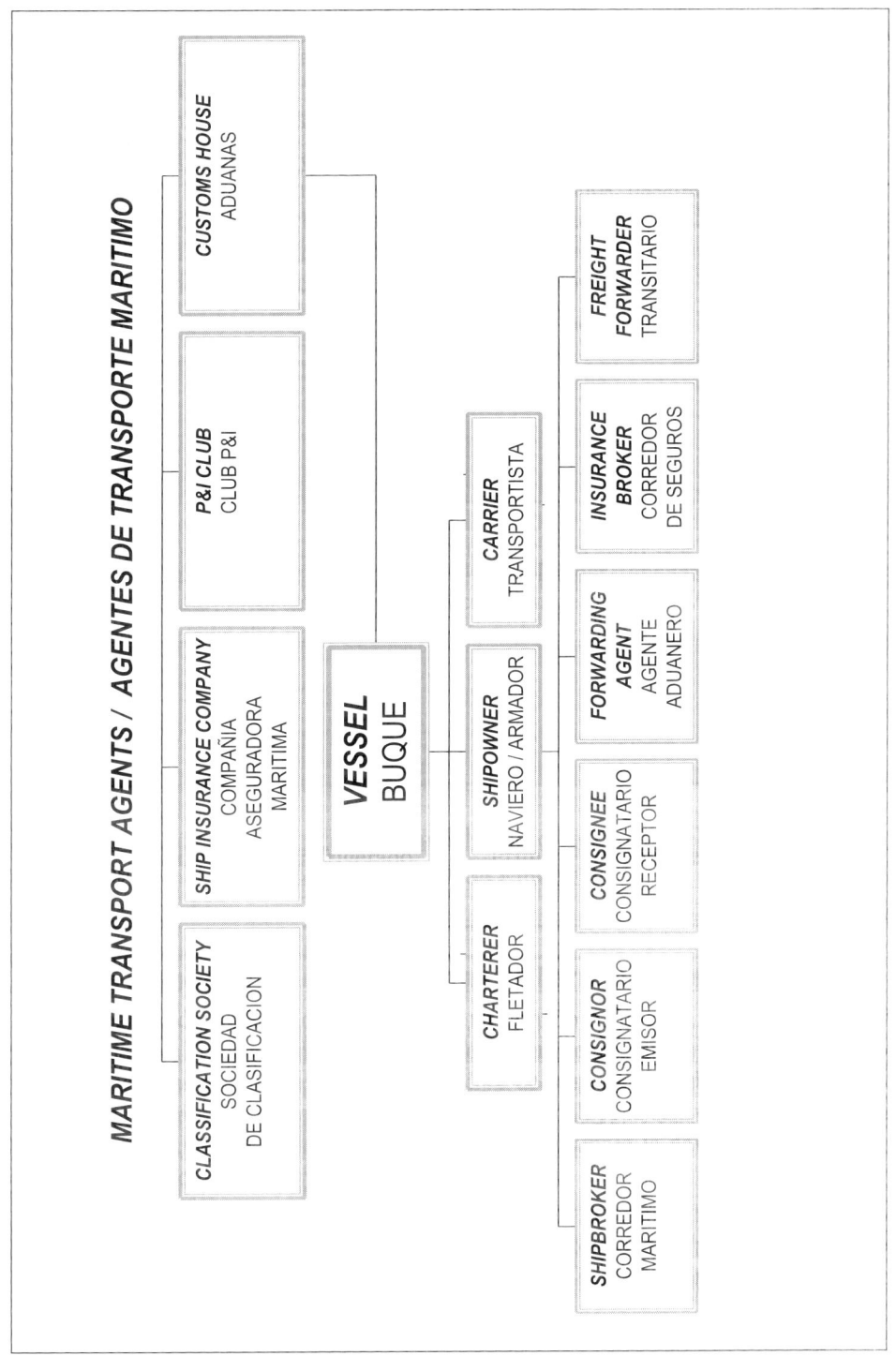

4
Contratos del transporte marítimo

Introducción

En este capítulo se muestran distintos modelos de contratos en uso utilizados para el transporte marítimo, en los que se especifica la función de cada uno de ellos. Se incluyen tanto contratos entre fletante y fletador para el transporte de mercancía, como contratos entre armador y puerto, o armador y compañías aseguradoras.

La mayoría de los modelos o formularios utilizados en el comercio del transporte marítimo siguen una estructura similar, como se puede comprobar más adelante en los anexos. Los formularios constan de dos partes: la primera contiene las casillas donde se reflejan los datos de las partes contratantes y, la segunda, las cláusulas que rigen los contratos.

Entre los modelos reflejados, destacamos por un lado los contratos por pólizas de fletamento (*Charter Parties*), que se utilizan para el transporte de grandes mercancías, en el que intervienen un solo fletante y un solo fletador; y por otra parte, los contratos bajo conocimiento de embarque (*Bill of Lading*), modalidad propia del transporte en línea regular, en el que varios cargadores y receptores comparten un mismo buque y ruta, emitiéndose un conocimiento de embarque para cada caso.

1. *Charter Party* (Póliza de Fletamento)

En esta modalidad de contrato para el transporte de mercancía, los gastos de carga y descarga corren a cargo del fletante de acuerdo con las siguientes cláusulas:

- F.I. (*Free In*). Libre de gastos de carga.

- F.O. (*Free Out*). Libre de gastos de descarga.

- F.I.O. (*Free In and Out*). Libre de gastos de carga y descarga.

- F.I.O.S. (*Free In and Out and Stowed*). Libre de estiba y desestiba.

- F.I.L.O. (*Free In Liner Out*). Libre de gastos de estiba; los gastos de descarga en las mismas condiciones que el transporte en línea regular.

- L.I.F.O. (*Liner In Free Out*). Gastos de carga en las mismas condiciones que el transporte en línea regular, así como libre de gastos de desestiba.

- F.I.O.S.T. (*Free In and Out Stowed and Trimmed*). Incluye costes de estibaje y arrumaje.

- F.I.O.S.T.L.S.D. (*Free In and Out Stowed, Trimmed, Lashed, Secured and Dunnaged*) Además de los anteriores, incluye los costes de trincaje.

- LINER (*Liner Terms*). Las maniobras de estiba y desestiba corren por cuenta del buque o naviera. Es la condición más común en el caso del transporte de contenedores.

Existe otra cláusula F.I. (*Free In*), poco utilizada, en la que se acuerda que los gastos relativos a la carga de mercancía no corren a cargo del fletante. Es un proceso más complicado, en el que las operaciones portuarias se descomponen en varias etapas o fases. La aplicación de esta cláusula obedece, sobre todo, a los usos y costumbres de cada puerto y tráfico.

El contrato comienza cuando el capitán del buque notifica al fletador que el buque está en el lugar convenido y listo para recibir la carga; esto lo hace mediante el envío de la Carta de Alistamiento/Notificación de Arribo o *Notice of Readiness (NOR)*. Esta nota indicará el punto de partida de los plazos acordados para cargar (tiempo de plancha o *laytime/laydays*).

MODELO DE *NOTICE OF READINESS*

Name of the Shipping Company

Shipping Company Address

To:

*I, _____ (name of the master), master of the m.v._____
_____(name of the vessel), hereby certify that my vessel arrived at _____ (port of discharge) on _____ (date) at _____ (hour) and is in every way ready to load cargo.*

Signed _____ _____ (master)

Notice received on _____ (date) at _____ (time)
Notice accepted on _____ (date) at _____ (time)

Signed _____ (receiver)

MODELO DE CARTA DE ALISTAMIENTO/NOTIFICACIÓN DE ARRIBO

Nombre de la Compañía Naviera

Dirección de la Compañía Naviera

Para:

Yo, _____ (nombre del capitán), capitán del buque. _____ (nombre del buque), por la presente certifico que mi buque llegó a _____ (puerto de descarga) el _____ (fecha) a _____ (hora) y está preparado para cargar la mercancía.

Firmado _____ _____ (capitán)

Nota recibida el _____ (fecha) a _____ (hora)
Nota aceptada el _____ (fecha) a _____ (hora)

Firmada _____ (destinatario)

La estadía de un buque en puerto, o tiempo de plancha, para su carga comienza cuando se acepta la *notice of readiness*.

Posteriormente la Autoridad Portuaria emite el *Statement of Facts* (Estado de Hechos) en el que se refleja por orden cronológico el día y la hora de entrada del buque en puerto, la fecha de emisión del NOR, la fecha de comienzo y finalización de las operaciones, y la fecha de salida del buque; con este documento se obtiene la información para el cálculo del tiempo de plancha y, en su caso, las demoras.

1. Agents	STANDARD STATEMENTS OF FACTS (SHORT FORM)	
2. Vessel's name	3. Port	
4. Owners/Disponent Owners	5. Vessel berthed	
	6. Loading commenced	7. Loading completed
8. Cargo	9. Discharging commenced	10. Discharging completed
	11. Cargo documents on board	12. Vessel sailed
13. Charter Party*	14. Working hours/meal hours of the port*	
15. Bill of Lading weight/quantity 16. Outturn weight/quantity		
17. Vessel arrived on roads	18.	
19. Notice of readiness tendered	20.	
21. Next tide available	22.	

DETAILS OF DAILY WORKING*

Date	Day	Hours worked		Hours stopped		No. of gangs	Quantity load./disch.	Remarks*
		From	to	From	to			

General remarks*

Place and date	Name and signature (Master)*
Name and signature (Agents)*	Name and signature (for the Charterers/Shippers/Receivers)*

* See Explanatory Notes overleaf for filling in the boxes

INSTRUCTIONS FOR FILLING IN THE BOXES

General

It is recommended to fill in the boxes with a short text. When it is a matter of figures to be inserted as is the case in most of the boxes, this should be done as follows:

> 6. Loading commenced
> 1975-03-15-0800

the figures being mentioned in the following order: year-month-date-time.

Boxes Calling for Special Attention

Charter Party*:

Insert name and date of charter, for instance, "Gencon" dated 1975-03-01.

Working hours/meal hours of the port*:

Indicate normal working hours/meal hours of the port and not the actual hours worked on board the vessel which may be longer or shorter than the hours normally worked in the port. Such day-by-day figures should be indicated in the box provided for under "Details of Daily Working".

Some empty boxes are made available in which other relevant information applying to the particular port or vessel could be inserted, such as, time of granting free pratique, if applicable, etc.

Details of Daily Working*:

Insert day-by-day figures and indicate in the vertical column marked "Remarks * " all relevant details as to reasons for stoppages such as bad weather, strikes, breakdown of winches/cranes, shortage of cargo, etc.

General Remarks*:

This box should be used for insertion of such general observations which are not covered in any of the boxes provided for in the first main group of boxes, for instance, reasons for berthing delay or other general observations.

Signatures*:

It is of importance that the boxes provided for signatures are duly signed by the parties concerned.

En el cómputo del tiempo de plancha se utilizan los siguientes términos:

- *Running Days*: Días corridos o naturales.

- *Working Days (WD)*: Días laborables. Periodo de 24 horas de 00.00 a 00.00, aunque el trabajo no se realice las 24 horas. Este concepto incluye los domingos si es un día de trabajo habitual en el puerto en cuestión.

- *Working day of 24 hours*: Periodo de 24 horas, aunque éste comprenda dos días.

- *Sundays and Holidays Excepted (SHEX)*: Excluye domingos y festivos. Estos días no se tienen en cuenta incluso si se trabaja, cuando así se ha acordado entre el capitán (*master*) y el fletador (*charterer*). No obstante, la *Charter Party* puede especificar que estos días no se cuentan a menos que sean utilizados.

- *Sundays and Holidays Included (SHINC)*: Incluye domingos y festivos.

- *Weather Permitting (WP)*: Días en que las condiciones atmosféricas impiden operar.

- *Weather Working Days (WWD)*: Días laborables si el tiempo lo permite.

- *Weather Working Days of 24 Consecutive Hours*: Días laborables de 24 horas si el tiempo lo permite.

1.1. Clasificación

Las pólizas de fletamento se clasifican en función de las condiciones del contrato: el contrato de arrendamiento o fletamento a casco desnudo, es decir, sin tripulación (*Demise/Bareboat Charter*), el fletamento por viaje (*Voyage Charter*), y el fletamento por tiempo (*Time Charter*).

A) Demise/Bareboat Charter

Este contrato estipula que el armador/propietario del buque cede a un arrendatario la explotación y utilización de un buque por un periodo de tiempo determinado a cambio de un precio.

El arrendatario se convierte en armador temporal, realizando las gestiones tanto náuticas (conducción, manejo técnico …), como económicas (aprovechamiento comercial del buque).

A continuación presentamos un ejemplo de este modelo de contrato.

1. Shipbroker	**STANDARD BAREBOAT CHARTER** **CODE NAME: "BARECON 2001"** PART I
	2. Place and date
3. Owners/Place of business (Cl. 1)	4. Bareboat Charterers/Place of business (Cl. 1)
5. Vessel's name, call sign and flag (Cl. 1 and 3)	
6. Type of Vessel	7. GT/NT
8. When/Where built	9. Total DWT (abt.) in metric tons on summer freeboard
10. Classification Society (Cl. 3)	11. Date of last special survey by the Vessel's classification society
12. Further particulars of Vessel (also indicate minimum number of months' validity of class certificates agreed acc. to Cl. 3)	
13. Port or Place of delivery (Cl. 3)	14. Time for delivery (Cl. 4)
16. Port or Place of redelivery (Cl. 15)	17. No. of months' validity of trading and class certificates upon redelivery (Cl. 15)
18. Running days' notice if other than stated in Cl. 4	19. Frequency of dry-docking (Cl. 10(g))
20. Trading limits (Cl. 6)	
21. Charter period (Cl. 2)	22. Charter hire (Cl. 11)
23. New class and other safety requirements (state percentage of Vessel's insurance value acc. to Box 29)(Cl. 10(a)(ii))	
24. Rate of interest payable acc. to Cl. 11(f) and, if applicable, acc. to PART IV	25. Currency and method of payment (Cl. 11)

26. Place of payment; also state beneficiary and bank account (Cl. 11)	27. Bank guarantee/bond (sum and place)(Cl. 24)(optional)
28. Mortgage(s), if any (state whether 12(a) or (b) applies; if 12(b) applies state date of Financial Instrument and name of Mortgagee(s)/Place of business)(Cl. 12)	29. Insurance (hull and machinery and war risks)(state value acc. to Cl. 13(f) or, if applicable, acc. to Cl. 14(k))(also state if Cl. 14 applies)
30. Additional insurance cover, if any, for Owners' account limited to (Cl. 13(b) or, if applicable, Cl. 14(g))	31. Additional insurance cover, if any, for Charterers' account limited to (Cl. 13(b) or, if applicable, Cl. 14(g))
32. Latent defects (only to be filled in if period other than stated in Cl. 3)	33. Brokerage commission and to whom payable (Cl. 27)
34. Grace period (state number of clear banking days)(Cl. 28)	35. Dispute Resolution (state 30(a), 30(b) or 30(c); if 30(c) agreed Place of Arbitration <u>must</u> be stated (Cl. 30)
36. War cancellation (indicate countries agreed)(Cl. 26(f))	
37. Newbuilding Vessel (indicate with "yes" or "no" whether PART III applies)(optional)	38. Name and place of Builders (only to be filled in if PART III applies)
39. Vessel's Yard Building No. (only to be filled in if PART III applies)	40. Date of Building Contract (only to be filled in if PART III applies)
41. Liquidated damages and costs shall accrue to (state party acc. to Cl. 1) a) b) c)	
42. Hire/Purchase agreement (indicate with "yes" or "no" whether PART IV applies)(optional)	43. Bareboat Charter Registry (indicate "yes" or "no" whether PART V applies)(optional)
44. Flag and Country of the Bareboat Charter Registry (only to be filled in if PART V applies)	45. Country of the Underlying Registry (only to be filled in if PART V applies)
46. Number of additional clauses covering special provisions, if agreed	

PREAMBLE - It is mutually agreed that this Contract shall be performed subject to the conditions contained in this Charter which shall include PART I and PART II. In the event of a conflict of conditions, the provisions of PART I shall prevail over those of PART II to the extent of such conflict but no further. It is further mutually agreed that PART III and/or PART IV and/or PART V shall only apply and only form part of this Charter if expressly agreed and stated in the Boxes 37, 42 and 43. If PART III and/or PART IV and/or PART V apply, it is further agreed that in the event of a conflict of conditions, the provisions of PART I and PART II shall prevail over those of PART III and/or PART IV and/or PART V to the extent of such conflict but no further.

Signature (Owners)	Signature (Charterers)

PART II
"BARECON 2001" Standard Bareboat Charter

1. **Definitions**
In this Charter, the following terms shall have the meanings hereby assigned to them:
"*The Owners*" shall mean the party identified in Box 3;
"*The Charterers*" shall mean the party identified in Box 4;
"*The Vessel*" shall mean the vessel named in Box 5 and with particulars as stated in Boxes 6 to 12.
"*Financial Instrument*" means the mortgage, deed of covenant or other such financial security instrument as annexed to this Charter and stated in Box 28.

2. **Charter Period**
In consideration of the hire detailed in Box 22, the Owners have agreed to let and the Charterers have agreed to hire the Vessel for the period stated in Box 21 ("The Charter Period").

3. **Delivery**
(not applicable when Part III applies, as indicated in Box 37)
(a) The Owners shall before and at the time of delivery exercise due diligence to make the Vessel seaworthy and in every respect ready in hull, machinery and equipment for service under this Charter.
The Vessel shall be delivered by the Owners and taken over by the Charterers at the port or place indicated in Box 13 in such ready safe berth as the Charterers may direct.
(b) The Vessel shall be properly documented on delivery in accordance with the laws of the flag State indicated in Box 5 and the requirements of the classification society stated in Box 10. The Vessel upon delivery shall have her survey cycles up to date and trading and class certificates valid for at least the number of months agreed in Box 12.
(c) The delivery of the Vessel by the Owners and the taking over of the Vessel by the Charterers shall constitute a full performance by the Owners of all the Owners' obligations under this Clause 3, and thereafter the Charterers shall not be entitled to make or assert any claim against the Owners on account of any conditions, representations or warranties expressed or implied with respect to the Vessel but the Owners shall be liable for the cost of but not the repairs or renewals occasioned by latent defects in the Vessel, her machinery or appurtenances, existing at the time of delivery under this Charter, provided such defects have manifested themselves within twelve (12) months after delivery unless otherwise provided in Box 32.

4. **Time for Delivery**
(not applicable when Part III applies, as indicated in Box 37)
The Vessel shall not be delivered before the date indicated in Box 14 without the Charterers' consent and the Owners shall exercise due diligence to deliver the Vessel not later than the date indicated in Box 15. Unless otherwise agreed in Box 18, the Owners shall give the Charterers not less than thirty (30) running days' preliminary and not less than fourteen (14) running days' definite notice of the date on which the Vessel is expected to be ready for delivery.
The Owners shall keep the Charterers closely advised of possible changes in the Vessel's position.

5. **Cancelling**
(not applicable when Part III applies, as indicated in Box 37)
(a) Should the Vessel not be delivered latest by the cancelling date indicated in Box 15, the Charterers shall have the option of cancelling this Charter by giving the Owners notice of cancellation within thirty-six (36) running hours after the cancelling date stated in Box 15, failing which this Charter shall remain in full force and effect.
(b) If it appears that the Vessel will be delayed beyond the cancelling date, the Owners may, as soon as they are in a position to state with reasonable certainty the day on which the Vessel should be ready, give notice thereof to the Charterers asking whether they will exercise their option of cancelling, and the option must then be declared within one hundred and sixty-eight (168) running hours of the receipt by the Charterers of such notice or within thirty-six (36) running hours after the cancelling date, whichever is the earlier. If the Charterers do not then exercise their option of cancelling, the seventh day after the readiness date stated in the Owners' notice shall be substituted for the cancelling date indicated in Box 15 for the purpose of this Clause 5.
(c) Cancellation under this Clause 5 shall be without prejudice to any claim the Charterers may otherwise have on the Owners under this Charter.

6. **Trading Restrictions**
The Vessel shall be employed in lawful trades for the carriage of suitable lawful merchandise within the trading limits indicated in Box 20.
The Charterers undertake not to employ the Vessel or suffer the Vessel to be employed otherwise than in conformity with the terms of the contracts of insurance (including any warranties expressed or implied therein) without first obtaining the consent of the insurers to such employment and complying with such requirements as to extra premium or otherwise as the insurers may prescribe.
The Charterers also undertake not to employ the Vessel or suffer her employment in any trade or business which is forbidden by the law of any country to which the Vessel may sail or is otherwise illicit or in carrying illicit or prohibited goods or in any manner whatsoever which may render her liable to condemnation, destruction, seizure or confiscation.
Notwithstanding any other provisions contained in this Charter it is agreed that nuclear fuels or radioactive products or waste are specifically excluded from the cargo permitted to be loaded or carried under this Charter. This exclusion does not apply to radio-isotopes used or intended to be used for any industrial, commercial, agricultural, medical or scientific purposes provided the Owners' prior approval has been obtained to loading thereof.

7. **Surveys on Delivery and Redelivery**
(not applicable when Part III applies, as indicated in Box 37)
The Owners and Charterers shall each appoint surveyors for the purpose of determining and agreeing in writing the condition of the Vessel at the time of delivery and redelivery hereunder. The Owners shall bear all expenses of the On-hire Survey including loss of time, if any, and the Charterers shall bear all expenses of the Off-hire Survey including loss of time, if any, at the daily equivalent to the rate of hire or pro rata thereof.

8. **Inspection**
The Owners shall have the right at any time after giving reasonable notice to the Charterers to inspect or survey the Vessel or instruct a duly authorised surveyor to carry out such survey on their behalf:-
(a) to ascertain the condition of the Vessel and satisfy

PART II
"BARECON 2001" Standard Bareboat Charter

themselves that the Vessel is being properly repaired and maintained. The costs and fees for such inspection or survey shall be paid by the Owners unless the Vessel is found to require repairs or maintenance in order to achieve the condition so provided;

(b) in dry-dock if the Charterers have not dry-docked her in accordance with Clause 10(g). The costs and fees for such inspection or survey shall be paid by the Charterers; and

(c) for any other commercial reason they consider necessary (provided it does not unduly interfere with the commercial operation of the Vessel). The costs and fees for such inspection and survey shall be paid by the Owners.

All time used in respect of inspection, survey or repairs shall be for the Charterers' account and form part of the Charter Period.

The Charterers shall also permit the Owners to inspect the Vessel's log books whenever requested and shall whenever required by the Owners furnish them with full information regarding any casualties or other accidents or damage to the Vessel.

9. **Inventories, Oil and Stores**
A complete inventory of the Vessel's entire equipment, outfit including spare parts, appliances and of all consumable stores on board the Vessel shall be made by the Charterers in conjunction with the Owners on delivery and again on redelivery of the Vessel. The Charterers and the Owners, respectively, shall at the time of delivery and redelivery take over and pay for all bunkers, lubricating oil, unbroached provisions, paints, ropes and other consumable stores (excluding spare parts) in the said Vessel at the then current market prices at the ports of delivery and redelivery, respectively. The Charterers shall ensure that all spare parts listed in the inventory and used during the Charter Period are replaced at their expense prior to redelivery of the Vessel.

10. **Maintenance and Operation**
(a)(i) Maintenance and Repairs - During the Charter Period the Vessel shall be in the full possession and at the absolute disposal for all purposes of the Charterers and under their complete control in every respect. The Charterers shall maintain the Vessel, her machinery, boilers, appurtenances and spare parts in a good state of repair, in efficient operating condition and in accordance with good commercial maintenance practice and, except as provided for in Clause 14(l), if applicable, at their own expense they shall at all times keep the Vessel's Class fully up to date with the Classification Society indicated in Box 10 and maintain all other necessary certificates in force at all times.

(ii) New Class and Other Safety Requirements - In the event of any improvement, structural changes or new equipment becoming necessary for the continued operation of the Vessel by reason of new class requirements or by compulsory legislation costing (excluding the Charterers' loss of time) more than the percentage stated in Box 23, or if Box 23 is left blank, 5 per cent. of the Vessel's insurance value as stated in Box 29, then the extent, if any, to which the rate of hire shall be varied and the ratio in which the cost of compliance shall be shared between the parties concerned in order to achieve a reasonable distribution thereof as between the Owners and the Charterers having regard, inter alia, to the length of the period remaining under this Charter shall, in the absence of agreement, be referred to the dispute resolution method agreed in Clause 30.

(iii) Financial Security - The Charterers shall maintain financial security or responsibility in respect of third party liabilities as required by any government, including federal, state or municipal or other division or authority thereof, to enable the Vessel, without penalty or charge, lawfully to enter, remain at, or leave any port, place, territorial or contiguous waters of any country, state or municipality in performance of this Charter without any delay. This obligation shall apply whether or not such requirements have been lawfully imposed by such government or division or authority thereof.

The Charterers shall make and maintain all arrangements by bond or otherwise as may be necessary to satisfy such requirements at the Charterers' sole expense and the Charterers shall indemnify the Owners against all consequences whatsoever (including loss of time) for any failure or inability to do so.

(b) Operation of the Vessel - The Charterers shall at their own expense and by their own procurement man, victual, navigate, operate, supply, fuel and, whenever required, repair the Vessel during the Charter Period and they shall pay all charges and expenses of every kind and nature whatsoever incidental to their use and operation of the Vessel under this Charter, including annual flag State fees and any foreign general municipality and/or state taxes. The Master, officers and crew of the Vessel shall be the servants of the Charterers for all purposes whatsoever, even if for any reason appointed by the Owners.

Charterers shall comply with the regulations regarding officers and crew in force in the country of the Vessel's flag or any other applicable law.

(c) The Charterers shall keep the Owners and the mortgagee(s) advised of the intended employment, planned dry-docking and major repairs of the Vessel, as reasonably required.

(d) Flag and Name of Vessel - During the Charter Period, the Charterers shall have the liberty to paint the Vessel in their own colours, install and display their funnel insignia and fly their own house flag. The Charterers shall also have the liberty, with the Owners' consent, which shall not be unreasonably withheld, to change the flag and/or the name of the Vessel during the Charter Period. Painting and re-painting, instalment and re-instalment, registration and re-registration, if required by the Owners, shall be at the Charterers' expense and time.

(e) Changes to the Vessel – Subject to Clause 10(a)(ii), the Charterers shall make no structural changes in the Vessel or changes in the machinery, boilers, appurtenances or spare parts thereof without in each instance first securing the Owners' approval thereof. If the Owners so agree, the Charterers shall, if the Owners so require, restore the Vessel to its former condition before the termination of this Charter.

(f) Use of the Vessel's Outfit, Equipment and Appliances - The Charterers shall have the use of all outfit, equipment, and appliances on board the Vessel at the time of delivery, provided the same or their substantial equivalent shall be returned to the Owners on redelivery in the same good order and condition as when received, ordinary wear and tear excepted. The

PART II
"BARECON 2001" Standard Bareboat Charter

Charterers shall from time to time during the Charter Period replace such items of equipment as shall be so damaged or worn as to be unfit for use. The Charterers are to procure that all repairs to or replacement of any damaged, worn or lost parts or equipment be effected in such manner (both as regards workmanship and quality of materials) as not to diminish the value of the Vessel. The Charterers have the right to fit additional equipment at their expense and risk but the Charterers shall remove such equipment at the end of the period if requested by the Owners. Any equipment including radio equipment on hire on the Vessel at time of delivery shall be kept and maintained by the Charterers and the Charterers shall assume the obligations and liabilities of the Owners under any lease contracts in connection therewith and shall reimburse the Owners for all expenses incurred in connection therewith, also for any new equipment required in order to comply with radio regulations.

(g) <u>Periodical Dry-Docking</u> - The Charterers shall dry-dock the Vessel and clean and paint her underwater parts whenever the same may be necessary, but not less than once during the period stated in Box 19 or, if Box 19 has been left blank, every sixty (60) calendar months after delivery or such other period as may be required by the Classification Society or flag State.

11. Hire
(a) The Charterers shall pay hire due to the Owners punctually in accordance with the terms of this Charter in respect of which time shall be of the essence.
(b) The Charterers shall pay to the Owners for the hire of the Vessel a lump sum in the amount indicated in Box 22 which shall be payable not later than every thirty (30) running days in advance, the first lump sum being payable on the date and hour of the Vessel's delivery to the Charterers. Hire shall be paid continuously throughout the Charter Period.
(c) Payment of hire shall be made in cash without discount in the currency and in the manner indicated in Box 25 and at the place mentioned in Box 26.
(d) Final payment of hire, if for a period of less than thirty (30) running days, shall be calculated proportionally according to the number of days and hours remaining before redelivery and advance payment to be effected accordingly.
(e) Should the Vessel be lost or missing, hire shall cease from the date and time when she was lost or last heard of. The date upon which the Vessel is to be treated as lost or missing shall be ten (10) days after the Vessel was last reported or when the Vessel is posted as missing by Lloyd's, whichever occurs first. Any hire paid in advance to be adjusted accordingly.
(f) Any delay in payment of hire shall entitle the Owners to interest at the rate per annum as agreed in Box 24. If Box 24 has not been filled in, the three months interbank offered rate in London (LIBOR or its successor) for the currency stated in Box 25, as quoted by the British Bankers' Association (BBA) on the date when the hire fell due, increased by 2 per cent., shall apply.
(g) Payment of interest due under sub-clause 11(f) shall be made within seven (7) running days of the date of the Owners' invoice specifying the amount payable or, in the absence of an invoice, at the time of the next hire payment date.

12. Mortgage
(only to apply if Box 28 has been appropriately filled in)

*) **(a)** The Owners warrant that they have not effected any mortgage(s) of the Vessel and that they shall not effect any mortgage(s) without the prior consent of the Charterers, which shall not be unreasonably withheld.
*) **(b)** The Vessel chartered under this Charter is financed by a mortgage according to the Financial Instrument. The Charterers undertake to comply, and provide such information and documents to enable the Owners to comply, with all such instructions or directions in regard to the employment, insurances, operation, repairs and maintenance of the Vessel as laid down in the Financial Instrument or as may be directed from time to time during the currency of the Charter by the mortgagee(s) in conformity with the Financial Instrument. The Charterers confirm that, for this purpose, they have acquainted themselves with all relevant terms, conditions and provisions of the Financial Instrument and agree to acknowledge this in writing in any form that may be required by the mortgagee(s). The Owners warrant that they have not effected any mortgage(s) other than stated in Box 28 and that they shall not agree to any amendment of the mortgage(s) referred to in Box 28 or effect any other mortgage(s) without the prior consent of the Charterers, which shall not be unreasonably withheld.
*) *(Optional, Clauses 12(a) and 12(b) are alternatives; indicate alternative agreed in Box 28).*

13. Insurance and Repairs
(a) During the Charter Period the Vessel shall be kept insured by the Charterers at their expense against hull and machinery, war and Protection and Indemnity risks (and any risks against which it is compulsory to insure for the operation of the Vessel, including maintaining financial security in accordance with sub-clause 10(a)(iii)) in such form as the Owners shall in writing approve, which approval shall not be un-reasonably withheld. Such insurances shall be arranged by the Charterers to protect the interests of both the Owners and the Charterers and the mortgagee(s) (if any), and the Charterers shall be at liberty to protect under such insurances the interests of any managers they may appoint. Insurance policies shall cover the Owners and the Charterers according to their respective interests. Subject to the provisions of the Financial Instrument, if any, and the approval of the Owners and the insurers, the Charterers shall effect all insured repairs and shall undertake settlement and reimbursement from the insurers of all costs in connection with such repairs as well as insured charges, expenses and liabilities to the extent of coverage under the insurances herein provided for.
The Charterers also to remain responsible for and to effect repairs and settlement of costs and expenses incurred thereby in respect of all other repairs not covered by the insurances and/or not exceeding any possible franchise(s) or deductibles provided for in the insurances.
All time used for repairs under the provisions of sub-clause 13(a) and for repairs of latent defects according to Clause 3(c) above, including any deviation, shall be for the Charterers' account.
(b) If the conditions of the above insurances permit additional insurance to be placed by the parties, such cover shall be limited to the amount for each party set out in Box 30 and Box 31, respectively. The Owners or the Charterers as the case may be shall immediately furnish the other party with particulars of any additional

PART II
"BARECON 2001" Standard Bareboat Charter

insurance effected, including copies of any cover notes or policies and the written consent of the insurers of any such required insurance in any case where the consent of such insurers is necessary.

(c) The Charterers shall upon the request of the Owners, provide information and promptly execute such documents as may be required to enable the Owners to comply with the insurance provisions of the Financial Instrument.

(d) Subject to the provisions of the Financial Instrument, if any, should the Vessel become an actual, constructive, compromised or agreed total loss under the insurances required under sub-clause 13(a), all insurance payments for such loss shall be paid to the Owners who shall distribute the moneys between the Owners and the Charterers according to their respective interests. The Charterers undertake to notify the Owners and the mortgagee(s), if any, of any occurrences in consequence of which the Vessel is likely to become a total loss as defined in this Clause.

(e) The Owners shall upon the request of the Charterers, promptly execute such documents as may be required to enable the Charterers to abandon the Vessel to insurers and claim a constructive total loss.

(f) For the purpose of insurance coverage against hull and machinery and war risks under the provisions of sub-clause 13(a), the value of the Vessel is the sum indicated in Box 29.

14. Insurance, Repairs and Classification

(Optional, only to apply if expressly agreed and stated in Box 29, in which event Clause 13 shall be considered deleted).

(a) During the Charter Period the Vessel shall be kept insured by the Owners at their expense against hull and machinery and war risks under the form of policy or policies attached hereto. The Owners and/or insurers shall not have any right of recovery or subrogation against the Charterers on account of loss of or any damage to the Vessel or her machinery or appurtenances covered by such insurance, or on account of payments made to discharge claims against or liabilities of the Vessel or the Owners covered by such insurance. Insurance policies shall cover the Owners and the Charterers according to their respective interests.

(b) During the Charter Period the Vessel shall be kept insured by the Charterers at their expense against Protection and Indemnity risks (and any risks against which it is compulsory to insure for the operation of the Vessel, including maintaining financial security in accordance with sub-clause 10(a)(iii)) in such form as the Owners shall in writing approve which approval shall not be unreasonably withheld.

(c) In the event that any act or negligence of the Charterers shall vitiate any of the insurance herein provided, the Charterers shall pay to the Owners all losses and indemnify the Owners against all claims and demands which would otherwise have been covered by such insurance.

(d) The Charterers shall, subject to the approval of the Owners or Owners' Underwriters, effect all insured repairs, and the Charterers shall undertake settlement of all miscellaneous expenses in connection with such repairs as well as all insured charges, expenses and liabilities, to the extent of coverage under the insurances provided for under the provisions of sub-clause 14(a). The Charterers to be secured reimbursement through the Owners' Underwriters for such expenditures upon presentation of accounts.

(e) The Charterers to remain responsible for and to effect repairs and settlement of costs and expenses incurred thereby in respect of all other repairs not covered by the insurances and/or not exceeding any possible franchise(s) or deductibles provided for in the insurances.

(f) All time used for repairs under the provisions of sub-clauses 14(d) and 14(e) and for repairs of latent defects according to Clause 3 above, including any deviation, shall be for the Charterers' account and shall form part of the Charter Period.

The Owners shall not be responsible for any expenses as are incident to the use and operation of the Vessel for such time as may be required to make such repairs.

(g) If the conditions of the above insurances permit additional insurance to be placed by the parties such cover shall be limited to the amount for each party set out in Box 30 and Box 31, respectively. The Owners or the Charterers as the case may be shall immediately furnish the other party with particulars of any additional insurance effected, including copies of any cover notes or policies and the written consent of the insurers of any such required insurance in any case where the consent of such insurers is necessary.

(h) Should the Vessel become an actual, constructive, compromised or agreed total loss under the insurances required under sub-clause 14(a), all insurance payments for such loss shall be paid to the Owners, who shall distribute the moneys between themselves and the Charterers according to their respective interests.

(i) If the Vessel becomes an actual, constructive, compromised or agreed total loss under the insurances arranged by the Owners in accordance with sub-clause 14(a), this Charter shall terminate as of the date of such loss.

(j) The Charterers shall upon the request of the Owners, promptly execute such documents as may be required to enable the Owners to abandon the Vessel to the insurers and claim a constructive total loss.

(k) For the purpose of insurance coverage against hull and machinery and war risks under the provisions of sub-clause 14(a), the value of the Vessel is the sum indicated in Box 29.

(l) Notwithstanding anything contained in sub-clause 10(a), it is agreed that under the provisions of Clause 14, if applicable, the Owners shall keep the Vessel's Class fully up to date with the Classification Society indicated in Box 10 and maintain all other necessary certificates in force at all times.

15. Redelivery

At the expiration of the Charter Period the Vessel shall be redelivered by the Charterers to the Owners at a safe and ice-free port or place as indicated in Box 16, in such ready safe berth as the Owners may direct. The Charterers shall give the Owners not less than thirty (30) running days' preliminary notice of expected date, range of ports of redelivery or port or place of redelivery and not less than fourteen (14) running days' definite notice of expected date and port or place of redelivery. Any changes thereafter in the Vessel's position shall be notified immediately to the Owners.

The Charterers warrant that they will not permit the Vessel to commence a voyage (including any preceding ballast voyage) which cannot reasonably be expected to be completed in time to allow redelivery of the Vessel within the Charter Period. Notwithstanding the above,

PART II
"BARECON 2001" Standard Bareboat Charter

should the Charterers fail to redeliver the Vessel within the Charter Period, the Charterers shall pay the daily equivalent to the rate of hire stated in Box 22 plus 10 per cent. or to the market rate, whichever is the higher, for the number of days by which the Charter Period is exceeded. All other terms, conditions and provisions of this Charter shall continue to apply.
Subject to the provisions of Clause 10, the Vessel shall be redelivered to the Owners in the same or as good structure, state, condition and class as that in which she was delivered, fair wear and tear not affecting class excepted.
The Vessel upon redelivery shall have her survey cycles up to date and trading and class certificates valid for at least the number of months agreed in Box 17.

16. Non-Lien
The Charterers will not suffer, nor permit to be continued, any lien or encumbrance incurred by them or their agents, which might have priority over the title and interest of the Owners in the Vessel. The Charterers further agree to fasten to the Vessel in a conspicuous place and to keep so fastened during the Charter Period a notice reading as follows:
"This Vessel is the property of (name of Owners). It is under charter to (name of Charterers) and by the terms of the Charter Party neither the Charterers nor the Master have any right, power or authority to create, incur or permit to be imposed on the Vessel any lien whatsoever."

17. Indemnity
(a) The Charterers shall indemnify the Owners against any loss, damage or expense incurred by the Owners arising out of or in relation to the operation of the Vessel by the Charterers, and against any lien of whatsoever nature arising out of an event occurring during the Charter Period. If the Vessel be arrested or otherwise detained by reason of claims or liens arising out of her operation hereunder by the Charterers, the Charterers shall at their own expense take all reasonable steps to secure that within a reasonable time the Vessel is released, including the provision of bail.
Without prejudice to the generality of the foregoing, the Charterers agree to indemnify the Owners against all consequences or liabilities arising from the Master, officers or agents signing Bills of Lading or other documents.
(b) If the Vessel be arrested or otherwise detained by reason of a claim or claims against the Owners, the Owners shall at their own expense take all reasonable steps to secure that within a reasonable time the Vessel is released, including the provision of bail.
In such circumstances the Owners shall indemnify the Charterers against any loss, damage or expense incurred by the Charterers (including hire paid under this Charter) as a direct consequence of such arrest or detention.

18. Lien
The Owners to have a lien upon all cargoes, sub-hires and sub-freights belonging or due to the Charterers or any sub-charterers and any Bill of Lading freight for all claims under this Charter, and the Charterers to have a lien on the Vessel for all moneys paid in advance and not earned.

19. Salvage
All salvage and towage performed by the Vessel shall be for the Charterers' benefit and the cost of repairing damage occasioned thereby shall be borne by the Charterers.

20. Wreck Removal
In the event of the Vessel becoming a wreck or obstruction to navigation the Charterers shall indemnify the Owners against any sums whatsoever which the Owners shall become liable to pay and shall pay in consequence of the Vessel becoming a wreck or obstruction to navigation.

21. General Average
The Owners shall not contribute to General Average.

22. Assignment, Sub-Charter and Sale
(a) The Charterers shall not assign this Charter nor sub-charter the Vessel on a bareboat basis except with the prior consent in writing of the Owners, which shall not be unreasonably withheld, and subject to such terms and conditions as the Owners shall approve.
(b) The Owners shall not sell the Vessel during the currency of this Charter except with the prior written consent of the Charterers, which shall not be unreasonably withheld, and subject to the buyer accepting an assignment of this Charter.

23. Contracts of Carriage
*) (a) The Charterers are to procure that all documents issued during the Charter Period evidencing the terms and conditions agreed in respect of carriage of goods shall contain a paramount clause incorporating any legislation relating to carrier's liability for cargo compulsorily applicable in the trade; if no such legislation exists, the documents shall incorporate the Hague-Visby Rules. The documents shall also contain the New Jason Clause and the Both-to-Blame Collision Clause.
*) (b) The Charterers are to procure that all passenger tickets issued during the Charter Period for the carriage of passengers and their luggage under this Charter shall contain a paramount clause incorporating any legislation relating to carrier's liability for passengers and their luggage compulsorily applicable in the trade; if no such legislation exists, the passenger tickets shall incorporate the Athens Convention Relating to the Carriage of Passengers and their Luggage by Sea, 1974, and any protocol thereto.
*) *Delete as applicable.*

24. Bank Guarantee
(Optional, only to apply if Box 27 filled in)
The Charterers undertake to furnish, before delivery of the Vessel, a first class bank guarantee or bond in the sum and at the place as indicated in Box 27 as guarantee for full performance of their obligations under this Charter.

25. Requisition/Acquisition
(a) In the event of the Requisition for Hire of the Vessel by any governmental or other competent authority (hereinafter referred to as "Requisition for Hire") irrespective of the date during the Charter Period when "Requisition for Hire" may occur and irrespective of the length thereof and whether or not it be for an indefinite

PART II
"BARECON 2001" Standard Bareboat Charter

or a limited period of time, and irrespective of whether it may or will remain in force for the remainder of the Charter Period, this Charter shall not be deemed thereby or thereupon to be frustrated or otherwise terminated and the Charterers shall continue to pay the stipulated hire in the manner provided by this Charter until the time when the Charter would have terminated pursuant to any of the provisions hereof always provided however that in the event of "Requisition for Hire" any Requisition Hire or compensation received or receivable by the Owners shall be payable to the Charterers during the remainder of the Charter Period or the period of the "Requisition for Hire" whichever be the shorter.

(b) In the event of the Owners being deprived of their ownership in the Vessel by any Compulsory Acquisition of the Vessel or requisition for title by any governmental or other competent authority (hereinafter referred to as "Compulsory Acquisition"), then, irrespective of the date during the Charter Period when "Compulsory Acquisition" may occur, this Charter shall be deemed terminated as of the date of such "Compulsory Acquisition". In such event Charter Hire to be considered as earned and to be paid up to the date and time of such "Compulsory Acquisition".

26. War

(a) For the purpose of this Clause, the words "War Risks" shall include any war (whether actual or threatened), act of war, civil war, hostilities, revolution, rebellion, civil commotion, warlike operations, the laying of mines (whether actual or reported), acts of piracy, acts of terrorists, acts of hostility or malicious damage, blockades (whether imposed against all vessels or imposed selectively against vessels of certain flags or ownership, or against certain cargoes or crews or otherwise howsoever), by any person, body, terrorist or political group, or the Government of any state whatsoever, which may be dangerous or are likely to be or to become dangerous to the Vessel, her cargo, crew or other persons on board the Vessel.

(b) The Vessel, unless the written consent of the Owners be first obtained, shall not continue to or go through any port, place, area or zone (whether of land or sea), or any waterway or canal, where it reasonably appears that the Vessel, her cargo, crew or other persons on board the Vessel, in the reasonable judgement of the Owners, may be, or are likely to be, exposed to War Risks. Should the Vessel be within any such place as aforesaid, which only becomes dangerous, or is likely to be or to become dangerous, after her entry into it, the Owners shall have the right to require the Vessel to leave such area.

(c) The Vessel shall not load contraband cargo, or to pass through any blockade, whether such blockade be imposed on all vessels, or is imposed selectively in any way whatsoever against vessels of certain flags or ownership, or against certain cargoes or crews or otherwise howsoever, or to proceed to an area where she shall be subject, or is likely to be subject to a belligerent's right of search and/or confiscation.

(d) If the insurers of the war risks insurance, when Clause 14 is applicable, should require payment of premiums and/or calls because, pursuant to the Charterers' orders, the Vessel is within, or is due to enter and remain within, any area or areas which are specified by such insurers as being subject to additional premiums because of War Risks, then such premiums and/or calls shall be reimbursed by the Charterers to the Owners at the same time as the next payment of hire is due.

(e) The Charterers shall have the liberty:
(i) to comply with all orders, directions, recommendations or advice as to departure, arrival, routes, sailing in convoy, ports of call, stoppages, destinations, discharge of cargo, delivery, or in any other way whatsoever, which are given by the Government of the Nation under whose flag the Vessel sails, or any other Government, body or group whatsoever acting with the power to compel compliance with their orders or directions;
(ii) to comply with the orders, directions or recommendations of any war risks underwriters who have the authority to give the same under the terms of the war risks insurance;
(iii) to comply with the terms of any resolution of the Security Council of the United Nations, any directives of the European Community, the effective orders of any other Supranational body which has the right to issue and give the same, and with national laws aimed at enforcing the same to which the Owners are subject, and to obey the orders and directions of those who are charged with their enforcement.

(f) In the event of outbreak of war (whether there be a declaration of war or not) (i) between any two or more of the following countries: the United States of America; Russia; the United Kingdom; France; and the People's Republic of China, (ii) between any two or more of the countries stated in Box 36, both the Owners and the Charterers shall have the right to cancel this Charter, whereupon the Charterers shall redeliver the Vessel to the Owners in accordance with Clause 15, if the Vessel has cargo on board after discharge thereof at destination, or if debarred under this Clause from reaching or entering it at a near, open and safe port as directed by the Owners, or if the Vessel has no cargo on board, at the port at which the Vessel then is or if at sea at a near, open and safe port as directed by the Owners. In all cases hire shall continue to be paid in accordance with Clause 11 and except as aforesaid all other provisions of this Charter shall apply until redelivery.

27. Commission

The Owners to pay a commission at the rate indicated in Box 33 to the Brokers named in Box 33 on any hire paid under the Charter. If no rate is indicated in Box 33, the commission to be paid by the Owners shall cover the actual expenses of the Brokers and a reasonable fee for their work.

If the full hire is not paid owing to breach of the Charter by either of the parties the party liable therefor shall indemnify the Brokers against their loss of commission. Should the parties agree to cancel the Charter, the Owners shall indemnify the Brokers against any loss of commission but in such case the commission shall not exceed the brokerage on one year's hire.

28. Termination

(a) <u>Charterers' Default</u>
The Owners shall be entitled to withdraw the Vessel from the service of the Charterers and terminate the Charter with immediate effect by written notice to the Charterers if:
(i) the Charterers fail to pay hire in accordance with Clause 11. However, where there is a failure to make punctual payment of hire due to oversight, negligence, errors or omissions on the part of the

PART II
"BARECON 2001" Standard Bareboat Charter

Charterers or their bankers, the Owners shall give the Charterers written notice of the number of clear banking days stated in Box 34 (as recognised at the agreed place of payment) in which to rectify the failure, and when so rectified within such number of days following the Owners' notice, the payment shall stand as regular and punctual. Failure by the Charterers to pay hire within the number of days stated in Box 34 of their receiving the Owners' notice as provided herein, shall entitle the Owners to withdraw the Vessel from the service of the Charterers and terminate the Charter without further notice;

(ii) the Charterers fail to comply with the requirements of:
(1) Clause 6 (Trading Restrictions)
(2) Clause 13(a) (Insurance and Repairs)
provided that the Owners shall have the option, by written notice to the Charterers, to give the Charterers a specified number of days grace within which to rectify the failure without prejudice to the Owners' right to withdraw and terminate under this Clause if the Charterers fail to comply with such notice;

(iii) the Charterers fail to rectify any failure to comply with the requirements of sub-clause 10(a)(i) (Maintenance and Repairs) as soon as practically possible after the Owners have requested them in writing so to do and in any event so that the Vessel's insurance cover is not prejudiced.

(b) Owners' Default
If the Owners shall by any act or omission be in breach of their obligations under this Charter to the extent that the Charterers are deprived of the use of the Vessel and such breach continues for a period of fourteen (14) running days after written notice thereof has been given by the Charterers to the Owners, the Charterers shall be entitled to terminate this Charter with immediate effect by written notice to the Owners.

(c) Loss of Vessel
This Charter shall be deemed to be terminated if the Vessel becomes a total loss or is declared as a constructive or compromised or arranged total loss. For the purpose of this sub-clause, the Vessel shall not be deemed to be lost unless she has either become an actual total loss or agreement has been reached with her underwriters in respect of her constructive, compromised or arranged total loss or if such agreement with her underwriters is not reached it is adjudged by a competent tribunal that a constructive loss of the Vessel has occurred.

(d) Either party shall be entitled to terminate this Charter with immediate effect by written notice to the other party in the event of an order being made or resolution passed for the winding up, dissolution, liquidation or bankruptcy of the other party (otherwise than for the purpose of reconstruction or amalgamation) or if a receiver is appointed, or if it suspends payment, ceases to carry on business or makes any special arrangement or composition with its creditors.

(e) The termination of this Charter shall be without prejudice to all rights accrued due between the parties prior to the date of termination and to any claim that either party might have.

29. Repossession
In the event of the termination of this Charter in accordance with the applicable provisions of Clause 28, the Owners shall have the right to repossess the Vessel from the Charterers at her current or next port of call, or at a port or place convenient to them without hindrance or interference by the Charterers, courts or local authorities. Pending physical repossession of the Vessel in accordance with this Clause 29, the Charterers shall hold the Vessel as gratuitous bailee only to the Owners. The Owners shall arrange for an authorised representative to board the Vessel as soon as reasonably practicable following the termination of the Charter. The Vessel shall be deemed to be repossessed by the Owners from the Charterers upon the boarding of the Vessel by the Owners' representative. All arrangements and expenses relating to the settling of wages, disembarkation and repatriation of the Charterers' Master, officers and crew shall be the sole responsibility of the Charterers.

30. Dispute Resolution
*) (a) This Contract shall be governed by and construed in accordance with English law and any dispute arising out of or in connection with this Contract shall be referred to arbitration in London in accordance with the Arbitration Act 1996 or any statutory modification or re-enactment thereof save to the extent necessary to give effect to the provisions of this Clause.
The arbitration shall be conducted in accordance with the London Maritime Arbitrators Association (LMAA) Terms current at the time when the arbitration proceedings are commenced.
The reference shall be to three arbitrators. A party wishing to refer a dispute to arbitration shall appoint its arbitrator and send notice of such appointment in writing to the other party requiring the other party to appoint its own arbitrator within 14 calendar days of that notice and stating that it will appoint its arbitrator as sole arbitrator unless the other party appoints its own arbitrator and gives notice that it has done so within the 14 days specified. If the other party does not appoint its own arbitrator and give notice that it has done so within the 14 days specified, the party referring a dispute to arbitration may, without the requirement of any further prior notice to the other party, appoint its arbitrator as sole arbitrator and shall advise the other party accordingly. The award of a sole arbitrator shall be binding on both parties as if he had been appointed by agreement.
Nothing herein shall prevent the parties agreeing in writing to vary these provisions to provide for the appointment of a sole arbitrator.
In cases where neither the claim nor any counterclaim exceeds the sum of US$50,000 (or such other sum as the parties may agree) the arbitration shall be conducted in accordance with the LMAA Small Claims Procedure current at the time when the arbitration proceedings are commenced.

*) (b) This Contract shall be governed by and construed in accordance with Title 9 of the United States Code and the Maritime Law of the United States and any dispute arising out of or in connection with this Contract shall be referred to three persons at New York, one to be appointed by each of the parties hereto, and the third by the two so chosen; their decision or that of any two of them shall be final, and for the purposes of enforcing any award, judgement may be entered on an award by any court of competent jurisdiction. The proceedings shall be conducted in accordance with the rules of the Society of Maritime Arbitrators, Inc.
In cases where neither the claim nor any counterclaim

PART II
"BARECON 2001" Standard Bareboat Charter

exceeds the sum of US$50,000 (or such other sum as the parties may agree) the arbitration shall be conducted in accordance with the Shortened Arbitration Procedure of the Society of Maritime Arbitrators, Inc. current at the time when the arbitration proceedings are commenced.

*) **(c)** This Contract shall be governed by and construed in accordance with the laws of the place mutually agreed by the parties and any dispute arising out of or in connection with this Contract shall be referred to arbitration at a mutually agreed place, subject to the procedures applicable there.

(d) Notwithstanding (a), (b) or (c) above, the parties may agree at any time to refer to mediation any difference and/or dispute arising out of or in connection with this Contract.

In the case of a dispute in respect of which arbitration has been commenced under (a), (b) or (c) above, the following shall apply:-

(i) Either party may at any time and from time to time elect to refer the dispute or part of the dispute to mediation by service on the other party of a written notice (the "Mediation Notice") calling on the other party to agree to mediation.

(ii) The other party shall thereupon within 14 calendar days of receipt of the Mediation Notice confirm that they agree to mediation, in which case the parties shall thereafter agree a mediator within a further 14 calendar days, failing which on the application of either party a mediator will be appointed promptly by the Arbitration Tribunal ("the Tribunal") or such person as the Tribunal may designate for that purpose. The mediation shall be conducted in such place and in accordance with such procedure and on such terms as the parties may agree or, in the event of disagreement, as may be set by the mediator.

(iii) If the other party does not agree to mediate, that fact may be brought to the attention of the Tribunal and may be taken into account by the Tribunal when allocating the costs of the arbitration as between the parties.

(iv) The mediation shall not affect the right of either party to seek such relief or take such steps as it considers necessary to protect its interest.

(v) Either party may advise the Tribunal that they have agreed to mediation. The arbitration procedure shall continue during the conduct of the mediation but the Tribunal may take the mediation timetable into account when setting the timetable for steps in the arbitration.

(vi) Unless otherwise agreed or specified in the mediation terms, each party shall bear its own costs incurred in the mediation and the parties shall share equally the mediator's costs and expenses.

(vii) The mediation process shall be without prejudice and confidential and no information or documents disclosed during it shall be revealed to the Tribunal except to the extent that they are disclosable under the law and procedure governing the arbitration.

(Note: The parties should be aware that the mediation process may not necessarily interrupt time limits.)

(e) If Box 35 in Part I is not appropriately filled in, sub-clause 30(a) of this Clause shall apply. Sub-clause 30(d) shall apply in all cases.

*) *Sub-clauses 30(a), 30(b) and 30(c) are alternatives; indicate alternative agreed in Box 35.*

31. Notices

(a) Any notice to be given by either party to the other party shall be in writing and may be sent by fax, telex, registered or recorded mail or by personal service.

(b) The address of the Parties for service of such communication shall be as stated in Boxes 3 and 4 respectively.

B) Voyage Charter

Tipo de contrato en el que el fletante cede el buque al fletador por el tiempo de un viaje para su explotación comercial a cambio de un flete; en la cláusula 4 del formulario tipo se especifica que el pago de dicho flete puede realizarse por adelantado en base a la cantidad cargada *"intaken quantity"* o tras la entrega, en base a la cantidad recibida *"delivered quantity"*.

Ambas partes, fletante y fletador, además de las obligaciones a las que se compromete a la hora de realizar el contrato, es decir, entregar las mercancías en destino el primero, y pagar el flete pactado el segundo, ha de cumplir otras obligaciones. Por una parte, el fletante ha de garantizar la navegabilidad del buque (*seaworthiness*), especificando que cumple las condiciones de seguridad necesarias para transportar mercancías (*cargoworthiness*); es también esta figura la que se encarga de las actividades de carga, estiba, descarga y entrega de las mercancías. Por su parte, el fletador se encarga de poner a disposición del fletante la mercancía en el momento y lugar convenidos.

Al igual que en otros contratos, muchas de estas pólizas incluyen una cláusula mediante la cual se puede romper el acuerdo de mutuo acuerdo, extinguiéndose las obligaciones de ambos; pero también podría darse el caso de ruptura de contrato por voluntad de una sola parte por incumplimiento de los deberes por la otra parte, lo que supondría el pago de una compensación económica, calculada de forma que la parte afectada por el incumplimiento no resulte perjudicada con respecto a la situación en la que se encontraría si el contrato se hubiese cumplido; esta indemnización en ningún caso puede exceder el total del flete pactado.

Este contrato se utiliza habitualmente para el tráfico de mercancías a granel, sólidas o líquidas.

Aunque bajo este tipo de contrato existen formularios específicos para cada clase de mercancía, que se adaptan a los tráficos correspondientes, como pueden ser NORGRAIN o GRAINVOY (grano), SHELLVOY (combustible), COAL-OREVOY (carbón y minerales), etc., existe un formulario general, conocido como GENCON, aceptado por la Comunidad Marítima Internacional.

He aquí un ejemplo del formulario GENCON.

1. Shipbroker	RECOMMENDED THE BALTIC AND INTERNATIONAL MARITIME COUNCIL UNIFORM GENERAL CHARTER (AS REVISED 1922, 1976 and 1994) (To be used for trades for which no specially approved form is in force) CODE NAME: "GENCON"
	2. Place and date
3. Owners/Place of business (Cl. 1)	4. Charterers/Place of business (Cl. 1)
5. Vessel's name (Cl. 1)	6. GT/NT (Cl. 1)
7. DWT all told on summer load line in metric tons (abt.) (Cl. 1)	8. Present position (Cl. 1)
9. Expected ready to load (abt.) (Cl. 1)	
10. Loading port or place (Cl. 1)	11. Discharging port or place (Cl. 1)
12. Cargo (also state quantity and margin in Owners' option, if agreed; if full and complete cargo not agreed state "part cargo") (Cl. 1)	
13. Freight rate (also state whether freight prepaid or payable on delivery) (Cl. 4)	14. Freight payment (state currency and method of payment; also beneficiary and bank account) (Cl. 4)
15. State if vessel's cargo handling gear shall not be used (Cl. 5)	16. Laytime (if separate laytime for load. and disch. is agreed, fill in a) and b). If total laytime for load. and disch., fill in c) only) (Cl. 6)
17. Shippers/Place of business (Cl. 6)	a) Laytime for loading
18. Agents (loading) (Cl. 6)	b) Laytime for discharging
19. Agents (discharging) (Cl. 6)	c) Total laytime for loading and discharging
20. Demurrage rate and manner payable (loading and discharging) (Cl. 7)	21. Cancelling date (Cl. 9)
	22. General Average to be adjusted at (Cl. 12)
23. Freight Tax (state if for the Owners' account) (Cl. 13 (c))	24. Brokerage commission and to whom payable (Cl. 15)
25. Law and Arbitration (state 19 (a), 19 (b) or 19 (c) of Cl. 19; if 19 (c) agreed also state Place of Arbitration) (if not filled in 19 (a) shall apply) (Cl. 19)	
(a) State maximum amount for small claims/shortened arbitration (Cl. 19)	26. Additional clauses covering special provisions, if agreed

It is mutually agreed that this Contract shall be performed subject to the conditions contained in this Charter Party which shall include Part I as well as Part II. In the event of a conflict of conditions, the provisions of Part I shall prevail over those of Part II to the extent of such conflict.

Signature (Owners)	Signature (Charterers)

PART II
"Gencon" Charter (As Revised 1922, 1976 and 1994)

1. It is agreed between the party mentioned in Box 3 as the Owners of the Vessel named in Box 5, of the GT/NT indicated in Box 6 and carrying about the number of metric tons of deadweight capacity all told on summer loadline stated in Box 7, now in position as stated in Box 8 and expected ready to load under this Charter Party about the date indicated in Box 9, and the party mentioned as the Charterers in Box 4 that:
The said Vessel shall, as soon as her prior commitments have been completed, proceed to the loading port(s) or place(s) stated in Box 10 or so near thereto as she may safely get and lie always afloat, and there load a full and complete cargo (if shipment of deck cargo agreed same to be at the Charterers' risk and responsibility) as stated in Box 12, which the Charterers bind themselves to ship, and being so loaded the Vessel shall proceed to the discharging port(s) or place(s) stated in Box 11 as ordered on signing Bills of Lading, or so near thereto as she may safely get and lie always afloat, and there deliver the cargo.

2. **Owners' Responsibility Clause**
The Owners are to be responsible for loss of or damage to the goods or for delay in delivery of the goods only in case the loss, damage or delay has been caused by personal want of due diligence on the part of the Owners or their Manager to make the Vessel in all respects seaworthy and to secure that she is properly manned, equipped and supplied, or by the personal act or default of the Owners or their Manager.
And the Owners are not responsible for loss, damage or delay arising from any other cause whatsoever, even from the neglect or default of the Master or crew or some other person employed by the Owners on board or ashore for whose acts they would, but for this Clause, be responsible, or from unseaworthiness of the Vessel on loading or commencement of the voyage or at any time whatsoever.

3. **Deviation Clause**
The Vessel has liberty to call at any port or ports in any order, for any purpose, to sail without pilots, to tow and/or assist Vessels in all situations, and also to deviate for the purpose of saving life and/or property.

4. **Payment of Freight**
(a) The freight at the rate stated in Box 13 shall be paid in cash calculated on the intaken quantity of cargo.
(b) *Prepaid*. If according to Box 13 freight is to be paid on shipment, it shall be deemed earned and non-returnable, Vessel and/or cargo lost or not lost.
Neither the Owners nor their agents shall be required to sign or endorse bills of lading showing freight prepaid unless the freight due to the Owners has actually been paid.
(c) *On delivery*. If according to Box 13 freight, or part thereof, is payable at destination it shall not be deemed earned until the cargo is thus delivered. Notwithstanding the provisions under (a), if freight or part thereof is payable on delivery of the cargo the Charterers shall have the option of paying the freight on delivered weight/quantity provided such option is declared before breaking bulk and the weight/quantity can be ascertained by official weighing machine, joint draft survey or tally.
Cash for Vessel's ordinary disbursements at the port of loading to be advanced by the Charterers, if required, at highest current rate of exchange, subject to two (2) per cent to cover insurance and other expenses.

5. **Loading/Discharging**
(a) *Costs/Risks*
The cargo shall be brought into the holds, loaded, stowed and/or trimmed, tallied, lashed and/or secured and taken from the holds and discharged by the Charterers, free of any risk, liability and expense whatsoever to the Owners. The Charterers shall provide and lay all dunnage material as required for the proper stowage and protection of the cargo on board, the Owners allowing the use of all dunnage available on board. The Charterers shall be responsible for and pay the cost of removing their dunnage after discharge of the cargo under this Charter Party and time to count until dunnage has been removed.
(b) *Cargo Handling Gear*
Unless the Vessel is gearless or unless it has been agreed between the parties that the Vessel's gear shall not be used and stated as such in Box 15, the Owners shall throughout the duration of loading/discharging give free use of the Vessel's cargo handling gear and of sufficient motive power to operate all such cargo handling gear. All such equipment to be in good working order. Unless caused by negligence of the stevedores, time lost by breakdown of the Vessel's cargo handling gear or motive power - pro rata the total number of cranes/winches required at that time for the loading/discharging of cargo under this Charter Party - shall not count as laytime or time on demurrage.
On request the Owners shall provide free of charge cranemen/winchmen from the crew to operate the Vessel's cargo handling gear, unless local regulations prohibit this, in which latter event shore labourers shall be for the account of the Charterers. Cranemen/winchmen shall be under the Charterers' risk and responsibility and as stevedores to be deemed as their servants but shall always work under the supervision of the Master.
(c) *Stevedore Damage*
The Charterers shall be responsible for damage (beyond ordinary wear and tear) to any part of the Vessel caused by Stevedores. Such damage shall be notified as soon as reasonably possible by the Master to the Charterers or their agents and to their Stevedores, failing which the Charterers shall not be held responsible. The Master shall endeavour to obtain the Stevedores' written acknowledgement of liability.
The Charterers are obliged to repair any stevedore damage prior to completion of the voyage, but must repair stevedore damage affecting the Vessel's seaworthiness or class before the Vessel sails from the port where such damage was caused or found. All additional expenses incurred shall be for the account of the Charterers and any time lost shall be for the account of and shall be paid to the Owners by the Charterers at the demurrage rate.

6. **Laytime**
* (a) *Separate laytime for loading and discharging*
The cargo shall be loaded within the number of running days/hours as indicated in Box 16, weather permitting, Sundays and holidays excepted, unless used, in which event time used shall count.
The cargo shall be discharged within the number of running days/hours as indicated in Box 16, weather permitting, Sundays and holidays excepted, unless used, in which event time used shall count.
* (b) *Total laytime for loading and discharging*
The cargo shall be loaded and discharged within the number of total running days/hours as indicated in Box 16, weather permitting, Sundays and holidays excepted, unless used, in which event time used shall count.
(c) *Commencement of laytime (loading and discharging)*
Laytime for loading and discharging shall commence at 13.00 hours, if notice of readiness is given up to and including 12.00 hours, and at 06.00 hours next working day if notice given during office hours after 12.00 hours. Notice of readiness at loading port to be given to the Shippers named in Box 17 or if not named, to the Charterers or their agents named in Box 18. Notice of readiness at the discharging port to be given to the Receivers or, if not known, to the Charterers or their agents named in Box 19.
If the loading/discharging berth is not available on the Vessel's arrival at or off the port of loading/discharging, the Vessel shall be entitled to give notice of readiness within ordinary office hours on arrival there, whether in free pratique or not, whether customs cleared or not. Laytime or time on demurrage shall then count as if she were in berth and in all respects ready for loading/ discharging provided that the Master warrants that she is in fact ready in all respects. Time used in moving from the place of waiting to the loading/ discharging berth shall not count as laytime.
If, after inspection, the Vessel is found not to be ready in all respects to load/ discharge time lost after the discovery thereof until the Vessel is again ready to load/discharge shall not count as laytime.
Time used before commencement of laytime shall count.
* Indicate alternative (a) or (b) as agreed, in Box 16.

7. **Demurrage**
Demurrage at the loading and discharging port is payable by the Charterers at the rate stated in Box 20 in the manner stated in Box 20 per day or pro rata for any part of a day. Demurrage shall fall due day by day and shall be payable upon receipt of the Owners' invoice.
In the event the demurrage is not paid in accordance with the above, the Owners shall give the Charterers 96 running hours written notice to rectify the failure. If the demurrage is not paid at the expiration of this time limit and if the vessel is in or at the loading port, the Owners are entitled at any time to terminate the Charter Party and claim damages for any losses caused thereby.

8. **Lien Clause**
The Owners shall have a lien on the cargo and on all sub-freights payable in respect of the cargo, for freight, deadfreight, demurrage, claims for damages and for all other amounts due under this Charter Party including costs of recovering same.

9. **Cancelling Clause**
(a) Should the Vessel not be ready to load (whether in berth or not) on the cancelling date indicated in Box 21, the Charterers shall have the option of cancelling this Charter Party.
(b) Should the Owners anticipate that, despite the exercise of due diligence, the Vessel will not be ready to load by the cancelling date, they shall notify the Charterers thereof without delay stating the expected date of the Vessel's readiness to load and asking whether the Charterers will exercise their option of cancelling the Charter Party, or agree to a new cancelling date.
Such option must be declared by the Charterers within 48 running hours after the receipt of the Owners' notice. If the Charterers do not exercise their option of cancelling, then this Charter Party shall be deemed to be amended such that

PART II
"Gencon" Charter (As Revised 1922, 1976 and 1994)

the seventh day after the new readiness date stated in the Owners' notification to the Charterers shall be the new cancelling date.
The provisions of sub-clause (b) of this Clause shall operate only once, and in case of the Vessel's further delay, the Charterers shall have the option of cancelling the Charter Party as per sub-clause (a) of this Clause.

10. Bills of Lading
Bills of Lading shall be presented and signed by the Master as per the "Congenbill" Bill of Lading form, Edition 1994, without prejudice to this Charter Party, or by the Owners' agents provided written authority has been given by Owners to the agents, a copy of which is to be furnished to the Charterers. The Charterers shall indemnify the Owners against all consequences or liabilities that may arise from the signing of bills of lading as presented to the extent that the terms or contents of such bills of lading impose or result in the imposition of more onerous liabilities upon the Owners than those assumed by the Owners under this Charter Party.

11. Both-to-Blame Collision Clause
If the Vessel comes into collision with another vessel as a result of the negligence of the other vessel and any act, neglect or default of the Master, Mariner, Pilot or the servants of the Owners in the navigation or in the management of the Vessel, the owners of the cargo carried hereunder will indemnify the Owners against all loss or liability to the other or non-carrying vessel or her owners in so far as such loss or liability represents loss of, or damage to, or any claim whatsoever of the owners of said cargo, paid or payable by the other or non-carrying vessel or her owners to the owners of said cargo and set-off, recouped or recovered by the other or non-carrying vessel or her owners as part of their claim against the carrying Vessel or the Owners. The foregoing provisions shall also apply where the owners, operators or those in charge of any vessel or vessels or objects other than, or in addition to, the colliding vessels or objects are at fault in respect of a collision or contact.

12. General Average and New Jason Clause
General Average shall be adjusted in London unless otherwise agreed in Box 22 according to York-Antwerp Rules 1994 and any subsequent modification thereof. Proprietors of cargo to pay the cargo's share in the general expenses even if same have been necessitated through neglect or default of the Owners' servants (see Clause 2).
If General Average is to be adjusted in accordance with the law and practice of the United States of America, the following Clause shall apply: "In the event of accident, danger, damage or disaster before or after the commencement of the voyage, resulting from any cause whatsoever, whether due to negligence or not, for which, or for the consequence of which, the Owners are not responsible, by statute, contract or otherwise, the cargo shippers, consignees or the owners of the cargo shall contribute with the Owners in General Average to the payment of any sacrifices, losses or expenses of a General Average nature that may be made or incurred and shall pay salvage and special charges incurred in respect of the cargo. If a salving vessel is owned or operated by the Owners, salvage shall be paid for as fully as if the said salving vessel or vessels belonged to strangers. Such deposit as the Owners, or their agents, may deem sufficient to cover the estimated contribution of the goods and any salvage and special charges thereon shall, if required, be made by the cargo, shippers, consignees or owners of the goods to the Owners before delivery.".

13. Taxes and Dues Clause
(a) *On Vessel* -The Owners shall pay all dues, charges and taxes customarily levied on the Vessel, howsoever the amount thereof may be assessed.
(b) *On cargo* -The Charterers shall pay all dues, charges, duties and taxes customarily levied on the cargo, howsoever the amount thereof may be assessed.
(c) *On freight* -Unless otherwise agreed in Box 23, taxes levied on the freight shall be for the Charterers' account.

14. Agency
In every case the Owners shall appoint their own Agent both at the port of loading and the port of discharge.

15. Brokerage
A brokerage commission at the rate stated in Box 24 on the freight, dead-freight and demurrage earned is due to the party mentioned in Box 24.
In case of non-execution 1/3 of the brokerage on the estimated amount of freight to be paid by the party responsible for such non-execution to the Brokers as indemnity for the latter's expenses and work. In case of more voyages the amount of indemnity to be agreed.

16. General Strike Clause
(a) If there is a strike or lock-out affecting or preventing the actual loading of the cargo, or any part of it, when the Vessel is ready to proceed from her last port or at any time during the voyage to the port or ports of loading or after her arrival there, the Master or the Owners may ask the Charterers to declare, that they agree to reckon the laydays as if there were no strike or lock-out. Unless the Charterers have given such declaration in writing (by telegram, if necessary) within 24 hours, the Owners shall have the option of cancelling this Charter Party. If part cargo has already been loaded, the Owners must proceed with same, (freight payable on loaded quantity only) having liberty to complete with other cargo on the way for their own account.
(b) If there is a strike or lock-out affecting or preventing the actual discharging of the cargo on or after the Vessel's arrival at or off port of discharge and same has not been settled within 48 hours, the Charterers shall have the option of keeping the Vessel waiting until such strike or lock-out is at an end against paying half demurrage after expiration of the time provided for discharging until the strike or lock-out terminates and thereafter full demurrage shall be payable until the completion of discharging, or of ordering the Vessel to a safe port where she can safely discharge without risk of being detained by strike or lock-out. Such orders to be given within 48 hours after the Master or the Owners have given notice to the Charterers of the strike or lock-out affecting the discharge. On delivery of the cargo at such port, all conditions of this Charter Party and of the Bill of Lading shall apply and the Vessel shall receive the same freight as if she had discharged at the original port of destination, except that if the distance to the substituted port exceeds 100 nautical miles, the freight on the cargo delivered at the substituted port to be increased in proportion.
(c) Except for the obligations described above, neither the Charterers nor the Owners shall be responsible for the consequences of any strikes or lock-outs preventing or affecting the actual loading or discharging of the cargo.

17. War Risks ("Voywar 1993")
(1) For the purpose of this Clause, the words:
(a) The "Owners" shall include the shipowners, bareboat charterers, disponent owners, managers or other operators who are charged with the management of the Vessel, and the Master; and
(b) "War Risks" shall include any war (whether actual or threatened), act of war, civil war, hostilities, revolution, rebellion, civil commotion, warlike operations, the laying of mines (whether actual or reported), acts of piracy, acts of terrorists, acts of hostility or malicious damage, blockades (whether imposed against all Vessels or imposed selectively against Vessels of certain flags or ownership, or against certain cargoes or crews or otherwise howsoever), by any person, body, terrorist or political group, or the Government of any state whatsoever, which, in the reasonable judgement of the Master and/or the Owners, may be dangerous or are likely to be or to become dangerous to the Vessel, her cargo, crew or other persons on board the Vessel.
(2) If at any time before the Vessel commences loading, it appears that, in the reasonable judgement of the Master and/or the Owners, performance of the Contract of Carriage, or any part of it, may expose, or is likely to expose, the Vessel, her cargo, crew or other persons on board the Vessel to War Risks, the Owners may give notice to the Charterers cancelling this Contract of Carriage, or may refuse to perform such part of it as may expose, or may be likely to expose, the Vessel, her cargo, crew or other persons on board the Vessel to War Risks; provided always that if this Contract of Carriage provides that loading or discharging is to take place within a range of ports, and at the port or ports nominated by the Charterers the Vessel, her cargo, crew, or other persons onboard the Vessel may be exposed, or may be likely to be exposed, to War Risks, the Owners shall first require the Charterers to nominate any other safe port which lies within the range for loading or discharging, and may only cancel this Contract of Carriage if the Charterers shall not have nominated such safe port or ports within 48 hours of receipt of notice of such requirement.
(3) The Owners shall not be required to continue to load cargo for any voyage, or to sign Bills of Lading for any port or place, or to proceed or continue on any voyage, or on any part thereof, or to proceed through any canal or waterway, or to proceed to or remain at any port or place whatsoever, where it appears, either after the loading of the cargo commences, or at any stage of the voyage thereafter before the discharge of the cargo is completed, that, in the reasonable judgement of the Master and/or the Owners, the Vessel, her cargo (or any part thereof), crew or other persons on board the Vessel (or any one or more of them) may be, or are likely to be, exposed to War Risks. If it should so appear, the Owners may by notice request the Charterers to nominate a safe port for the discharge of the cargo or any part thereof, and if within 48 hours of the receipt of such notice, the Charterers shall not have nominated such a port, the Owners may discharge the cargo at any safe port of their choice (including the port of loading) in complete fulfilment of the Contract of Carriage. The Owners shall be entitled to recover from the Charterers the extra expenses of such discharge and, if the discharge takes place at any port other than the loading port, to receive the full freight as though the cargo had been

PART II
"Gencon" Charter (As Revised 1922, 1976 and 1994)

carried to the discharging port and if the extra distance exceeds 100 miles, to additional freight which shall be the same percentage of the freight contracted for as the percentage which the extra distance represents to the distance of the normal and customary route, the Owners having a lien on the cargo for such expenses and freight.

(4) If at any stage of the voyage after the loading of the cargo commences, it appears that, in the reasonable judgement of the Master and/or the Owners, the Vessel, her cargo, crew or other persons on board the Vessel may be, or are likely to be, exposed to War Risks on any part of the route (including any canal or waterway) which is normally and customarily used in a voyage of the nature contracted for, and there is another longer route to the discharging port, the Owners shall give notice to the Charterers that this route will be taken. In this event the Owners shall be entitled, if the total extra distance exceeds 100 miles, to additional freight which shall be the same percentage of the freight contracted for as the percentage which the extra distance represents to the distance of the normal and customary route.

(5) The Vessel shall have liberty:-
(a) to comply with all orders, directions, recommendations or advice as to departure, arrival, routes, sailing in convoy, ports of call, stoppages, destinations, discharge of cargo, delivery or in any way whatsoever which are given by the Government of the Nation under whose flag the Vessel sails, or other Government to whose laws the Owners are subject, or any other Government which so requires, or any body or group acting with the power to compel compliance with their orders or directions;
(b) to comply with the orders, directions or recommendations of any war risks underwriters who have the authority to give the same under the terms of the war risks insurance;
(c) to comply with the terms of any resolution of the Security Council of the United Nations, any directives of the European Community, the effective orders of any other Supranational body which has the right to issue and give the same, and with national laws aimed at enforcing the same to which the Owners are subject, and to obey the orders and directions of those who are charged with their enforcement;
(d) to discharge at any other port any cargo or part thereof which may render the Vessel liable to confiscation as a contraband carrier;
(e) to call at any other port to change the crew or any part thereof or other persons on board the Vessel when there is reason to believe that they may be subject to internment, imprisonment or other sanctions;
(f) where cargo has not been loaded or has been discharged by the Owners under any provisions of this Clause, to load other cargo for the Owners' own benefit and carry it to any other port or ports whatsoever, whether backwards or forwards or in a contrary direction to the ordinary or customary route.

(6) If in compliance with any of the provisions of sub-clauses (2) to (5) of this Clause anything is done or not done, such shall not be deemed to be a deviation, but shall be considered as due fulfilment of the Contract of Carriage.

18. General Ice Clause
Port of loading
(a) In the event of the loading port being inaccessible by reason of ice when the Vessel is ready to proceed from her last port or at any time during the voyage or on the Vessel's arrival or in case frost sets in after the Vessel's arrival, the Master for fear of being frozen in is at liberty to leave without cargo, and this Charter Party shall be null and void.
(b) If during loading the Master, for fear of the Vessel being frozen in, deems it advisable to leave, he has liberty to do so with what cargo he has on board and to proceed to any other port or ports with option of completing cargo for the Owners' benefit for any port or ports including port of discharge. Any part cargo thus loaded under this Charter Party to be forwarded to destination at the Vessel's expense but against payment of freight, provided that no extra expenses be thereby caused to the Charterers, freight being paid on quantity delivered (in proportion if lumpsum), all other conditions as per this Charter Party.
(c) In case of more than one loading port, and if one or more of the ports are closed by ice, the Master or the Owners to be at liberty either to load the part cargo at the open port and fill up elsewhere for their own account as under section (b) or to declare the Charter Party null and void unless the Charterers agree to load full cargo at the open port.

Port of discharge
(a) Should ice prevent the Vessel from reaching port of discharge the Charterers shall have the option of keeping the Vessel waiting until the re-opening of navigation and paying demurrage or of ordering the Vessel to a safe and immediately accessible port where she can safely discharge without risk of detention by ice. Such orders to be given within 48 hours after the Master or the Owners have given notice to the Charterers of the impossibility of reaching port of destination.
(b) If during discharging the Master for fear of the Vessel being frozen in deems it advisable to leave, he has liberty to do so with what cargo he has on board and to proceed to the nearest accessible port where she can safely discharge.
(c) On delivery of the cargo at such port, all conditions of the Bill of Lading shall apply and the Vessel shall receive the same freight as if she had discharged at the original port of destination, except that if the distance of the substituted port exceeds 100 nautical miles, the freight on the cargo delivered at the substituted port to be increased in proportion.

19. Law and Arbitration
* (a) This Charter Party shall be governed by and construed in accordance with English law and any dispute arising out of this Charter Party shall be referred to arbitration in London in accordance with the Arbitration Acts 1950 and 1979 or any statutory modification or re-enactment thereof for the time being in force. Unless the parties agree upon a sole arbitrator, one arbitrator shall be appointed by each party and the arbitrators so appointed shall appoint a third arbitrator, the decision of the three-man tribunal thus constituted or any two of them, shall be final. On the receipt by one party of the nomination in writing of the other party's arbitrator, that party shall appoint their arbitrator within fourteen days, failing which the decision of the single arbitrator appointed shall be final.
For disputes where the total amount claimed by either party does not exceed the amount stated in Box 25** the arbitration shall be conducted in accordance with the Small Claims Procedure of the London Maritime Arbitrators Association.

* (b) This Charter Party shall be governed by and construed in accordance with Title 9 of the United States Code and the Maritime Law of the United States and should any dispute arise out of this Charter Party, the matter in dispute shall be referred to three persons at New York, one to be appointed by each of the parties hereto, and the third by the two so chosen; their decision or that of any two of them shall be final, and for purpose of enforcing any award, this agreement may be made a rule of the Court. The proceedings shall be conducted in accordance with the rules of the Society of Maritime Arbitrators, Inc..
For disputes where the total amount claimed by either party does not exceed the amount stated in Box 25** the arbitration shall be conducted in accordance with the Shortened Arbitration Procedure of the Society of Maritime Arbitrators, Inc..

* (c) Any dispute arising out of this Charter Party shall be referred to arbitration at the place indicated in Box 25, subject to the procedures applicable there. The laws of the place indicated in Box 25 shall govern this Charter Party.
(d) If Box 25 in Part 1 is not filled in, sub-clause (a) of this Clause shall apply.
* (a), (b) and (c) are alternatives; indicate alternative agreed in Box 25.
** *Where no figure is supplied in Box 25 in Part 1, this provision only shall be void but the other provisions of this Clause shall have full force and remain in effect.*

C) Time Charter

El armador (fletante) pone a disposición del fletador el buque por un tiempo determinado a cambio de un precio o flete. A diferencia del contrato de arrendamiento *"Demise/Bareboat Charter"*, la gestión náutica es asumida por el armador, mientras que el fletador se encarga de la explotación comercial para el transporte de mercancías.

El contrato comienza cuando se realiza la puesta a disposición del buque por parte del fletante (*delivery of the vessel*) en fecha y lugar convenidos; esta entrega se considera realizada:

- *A.P.S. Upon Arrival at Pilot Station.* Cuando el buque llega a la estación de prácticos del puerto.

- *T.I.P. Upontaking the Inbound Pilot.* Cuando el práctico de entrada sube a bordo.

- *D.O.P. Dropping the Outbound Pilot.* Cuando el práctico de salida abandona el buque.

Este tipo de contratos es utilizado generalmente por armadores que necesitan, durante un tiempo concreto, más buques de los que habitualmente poseen o utilizan; o por empresas pertenecientes al sector marítimo que se ocupan de transportar mercancías, sin tener que preocuparse de los aspectos relacionados con la navegación.

Los formularios más conocidos y utilizados en este tipo de contratos son el BALTIME, aprobado por la BIMCO en 1902, cuya última versión data de 1974; y el NYPE, aprobado en 1913 por el *New Cork Produce Exchange*, que ha sufrido distintas variaciones hasta su última versión de 1981, conocida como ASBATIME. A pesar de ser reconocidos a nivel internacional, es práctica habitual que estas pólizas puedan variar en el caso de situaciones específicas.

En estas pólizas el fletante tiene, entre otras, las obligaciones de poner el buque a disposición del fletador en el lugar y momento convenidos, realizar los viajes decididos por el fletador durante el tiempo que dure el contrato, y abonar los gastos originados por la gestión náutica que incluye todos los gastos fijos como salarios de la tripulación, aranceles, seguro, reparaciones, etc. Por su parte, el fletador ha de correr con los gastos originados por la gestión comercial (combustible, tasas portuarias, gastos de remolcaje, etc.), pagar el flete y devolver el buque en el lugar y tiempo pactados.

A continuación se muestra un modelo de BALTIME.

1. Shipbroker	**TIME-CHARTER** **(AS REVISED 2001)** **CODE NAME: "BALTIME 1939"**
	2. Place and Date of Charter
3. Owners/Place of business	4. Charterers/Place of business
5. Vessel's Name	6. GT/NT
7. Class	8. Indicated brake horse power (bhp)
9. Total tons d.w. (abt.) on summer freeboard	10. Cubic feet grain/bale capacity
11. Permanent bunkers (abt.)	12. Speed capability in knots (abt.) on a consumption in tons (abt.) of
13. Present position	14. Period of hire (Cl. 1)
15. Port of delivery (Cl. 1)	16. Time of delivery (Cl. 1)
17. (a) Trade limits (Cl. 2) (b) Cargo exclusions specially agreed	
18. Bunkers on re-delivery (state min. and max. quantity)(Cl. 5)	19. Charter hire (Cl. 6)
20. Hire payment (state currency, method and place of payment; also beneficiary and bank account) (Cl. 6)	
21. Place or range of re-delivery (Cl. 7)	22. Cancelling date (Cl. 21)
23. Dispute resolution (state 22(A), 22(B) or 22(C); if 22(C) agreed Place of Arbitration <u>must</u> be stated) (Cl. 22)	24. Brokerage commission and to whom payable (Cl. 24)
25. Numbers of additional clauses covering special provisions, if agreed	

It is mutually agreed that this Contract shall be performed subject to the conditions contained in this Charter which shall include PART I as well as PART II. In the event of a conflict of conditions, the provisions of PART I shall prevail over those of PART II to the extent of such conflict.

Signature (Owners)	Signature (Charterers)

PART II
"BALTIME 1939" Uniform Time-Charter (as revised 2001)

It is agreed between the party mentioned in Box 3 as Owners of the Vessel named in Box 5 of the gross/net tonnage indicated in Box 6, classed as stated in Box 7 and of indicated brake horse power (bhp) as stated in Box 8, carrying about the number of tons deadweight indicated in Box 9 on summer freeboard inclusive of bunkers, stores and provisions, having as per builder's plan a cubic-feet grain/bale capacity as stated in Box 10, exclusive of permanent bunkers, which contain about the number of tons stated in Box 11, and fully loaded capable of steaming about the number of knots indicated in Box 12 in good weather and smooth water on a consumption of about the number of tons fuel oil stated in Box 12, now in position as stated in Box 13 and the party mentioned as Charterers in Box 4, as follows:

1. Period/Port of Delivery/Time of Delivery
The Owners let, and the Charterers hire the Vessel for a period of the number of calendar months indicated in Box 14 from the time (not a Sunday or a legal Holiday unless taken over) the Vessel is delivered and placed at the disposal of the Charterers between 9 a.m. and 6 p.m., or between 9 a.m. and 2 p.m. if on Saturday, at the port stated in Box 15 in such available berth where she can safely lie always afloat, as the Charterers may direct, the Vessel being in every way fitted for ordinary cargo service. The Vessel shall be delivered at the time indicated in Box 16.

2. Trade
The Vessel shall be employed in lawful trades for the carriage of lawful merchandise only between safe ports or places where the Vessel can safely lie always afloat within the limits stated in Box 17. No live stock nor injurious, inflammable or dangerous goods (such as acids, explosives, calcium carbide, ferro silicon, naphtha, motor spirit, tar, or any of their products) shall be shipped.

3. Owners' Obligations
The Owners shall provide and pay for all provisions and wages, for insurance of the Vessel, for all deck and engine-room stores and maintain her in a thoroughly efficient state in hull and machinery during service. The Owners shall provide winchmen from the crew to operate the Vessel's cargo handling gear, unless the crew's employment conditions or local union or port regulations prohibit this, in which case qualified shore-winchmen shall be provided and paid for by the Charterers.

4. Charterers' Obligations
The Charterers shall provide and pay for all fuel oil, port charges, pilotages (whether compulsory or not), canal steersmen, boatage, lights, tug-assistance, consular charges (except those pertaining to the Master, officers and crew), canal, dock and other dues and charges, including any foreign general municipality or state taxes, also all dock, harbour and tonnage dues at the ports of delivery and re-delivery (unless incurred through cargo carried before delivery or after re-delivery), agencies, commissions, also shall arrange and pay for loading, trimming, stowing (including dunnage and shifting boards, excepting any already on board), unloading, weighing, tallying and delivery of cargoes, surveys on hatches, meals supplied to officials and men in their service and all other charges and expenses whatsoever including detention and expenses through quarantine (including cost of fumigation and disinfection). All ropes, slings and special runners actually used for loading and discharging and any special gear, including special ropes and chains required by the custom of the port for mooring shall be for the Charterers' account. The Vessel shall be fitted with winches, derricks, wheels and ordinary runners capable of handling lifts up to 2 tons.

5. Bunkers
The Charterers at port of delivery and the Owners at port of re-delivery shall take over and pay for all fuel oil remaining in the Vessel's bunkers at current price at the respective ports. The Vessel shall be re-delivered with not less than the number of tons and not exceeding the number of tons of fuel oil in the Vessel's bunkers stated in Box 18.

6. Hire
The Charterers shall pay as hire the rate stated in Box 19 per 30 days, commencing in accordance with Clause 1 until her re-delivery to the Owners.
Payment of hire shall be made in cash, in the currency stated in Box 20, without discount, every 30 days, in advance, and in the manner prescribed in Box 20. In default of payment the Owners shall have the right of withdrawing the Vessel from the service of the Charterers, without noting any protest and without interference by any court or any other formality whatsoever and without prejudice to any claim the Owners may otherwise have on the Charterers under the Charter.

7. Re-delivery
The Vessel shall be re-delivered on the expiration of the Charter in the same good order as when delivered to the Charterers (fair wear and tear excepted) at an ice-free port in the Charterers' option at the place or within the range stated in Box 21, between 9 a.m. and 6 p.m., and 9 a.m. and 2 p.m. on Saturday, but the day of re-delivery shall not be a Sunday or legal Holiday.
The Charterers shall give the Owners not less than ten days' notice at which port and on about which day the Vessel will be re-delivered. Should the Vessel be ordered on a voyage by which the Charter period will be exceeded the Charterers shall have the use of the Vessel to enable them to complete the voyage, provided it could be reasonably calculated that the voyage would allow redelivery about the time fixed for the termination of the Charter, but for any time exceeding the termination date the Charterers shall pay the market rate if higher than the rate stipulated herein.

8. Cargo Space
The whole reach and burthen of the Vessel, including lawful deck-capacity shall be at the Charterers' disposal, reserving proper and sufficient space for the Vessel's Master, officers, crew, tackle, apparel, furniture, provisions and stores.

9. Master
The Master shall prosecute all voyages with the utmost despatch and shall render customary assistance with the Vessel's crew. The Master shall be under the orders of the Charterers as regards employment, agency, or other arrangements. The Charterers shall indemnify the Owners against all consequences or liabilities arising from the Master, officers or Agents signing Bills of Lading or other documents or otherwise complying with such orders, as well as from any irregularity in the Vessel's papers or for overcarrying goods. The Owners shall not be responsible for shortage, mixture, marks, nor for number of pieces or packages, nor for damage to or claims on cargo caused by bad stowage or otherwise. If

PART II
"BALTIME 1939" Uniform Time-Charter (as revised 2001)

the Charterers have reason to be dissatisfied with the conduct of the Master or any officer, the Owners, on receiving particulars of the complaint, promptly to investigate the matter, and, if necessary and practicable, to make a change in the appointments.

10. Directions and Logs
The Charterers shall furnish the Master with all instructions and sailing directions and the Master shall keep full and correct logs accessible to the Charterers or their Agents.

11. Suspension of Hire etc.
(A) In the event of drydocking or other necessary measures to maintain the efficiency of the Vessel, deficiency of men or Owners' stores, breakdown of machinery, damage to hull or other accident, either hindering or preventing the working of the Vessel and continuing for more than twenty-four consecutive hours, no hire shall be paid in respect of any time lost thereby during the period in which the Vessel is unable to perform the service immediately required. Any hire paid in advance shall be adjusted accordingly.
(B) In the event of the Vessel being driven into port or to anchorage through stress of weather, trading to shallow harbours or to rivers or ports with bars or suffering an accident to her cargo, any detention of the Vessel and/or expenses resulting from such detention shall be for the Charterers' account even if such detention and/or expenses, or the cause by reason of which either is incurred, be due to, or be contributed to by, the negligence of the Owners' servants.

12. Responsibility and Exemption
The Owners only shall be responsible for delay in delivery of the Vessel or for delay during the currency of the Charter and for loss or damage to goods onboard, if such delay or loss has been caused by want of due diligence on the part of the Owners or their Manager in making the Vessel seaworthy and fitted for the voyage or any other personal act or omission or default of the Owners or their Manager. The Owners shall not be responsible in any other case nor for damage or delay whatsoever and howsoever caused even if caused by the neglect or default of their servants. The Owners shall not be liable for loss or damage arising or resulting from strikes, lock-outs or stoppage or restraint of labour (including the Master, officers or crew) whether partial or general. The Charterers shall be responsible for loss or damage caused to the Vessel or to the Owners by goods being loaded contrary to the terms of the Charter or by improper or careless bunkering or loading, stowing or discharging of goods or any other improper or negligent act on their part or that of their servants.

13. Advances
The Charterers or their Agents shall advance to the Master, if required, necessary funds for ordinary disbursements for the Vessel's account at any port charging only interest at 6 per cent. p.a., such advances shall be deducted from hire.

14. Excluded Ports
The Vessel shall not be ordered to nor bound to enter:
(A) any place where fever or epidemics are prevalent or to which the Master, officers and crew by law are not bound to follow the Vessel;
(B) any ice-bound place or any place where lights, lightships, marks and buoys are or are likely to be withdrawn by reason of ice on the Vessel's arrival or where there is risk that ordinarily the Vessel will not be able on account of ice to reach the place or to get out after having completed loading or discharging. The Vessel shall not be obliged to force ice. If on account of ice the Master considers it dangerous to remain at the loading or discharging place for fear of the Vessel being frozen in and/or damaged, he has liberty to sail to a convenient open place and await the Charterers' fresh instructions. Unforeseen detention through any of above causes shall be for the Charterers' account.

15. Loss of Vessel
Should the Vessel be lost or missing, hire shall cease from the date when she was lost. If the date of loss cannot be ascertained half hire shall be paid from the date the Vessel was last reported until the calculated date of arrival at the destination. Any hire paid in advance shall be adjusted accordingly.

16. Overtime
The Vessel shall work day and night if required. The Charterers shall refund the Owners their outlays for all overtime paid to officers and crew according to the hours and rates stated in the Vessel's articles.

17. Lien
The Owners shall have a lien upon all cargoes and sub-freights belonging to the Time-Charterers and any Bill of Lading freight for all claims under this Charter, and the Charterers shall have a lien on the Vessel for all moneys paid in advance and not earned.

18. Salvage
All salvage and assistance to other vessels shall be for the Owners' and the Charterers' equal benefit after deducting the Master's, officers' and crew's proportion and all legal and other expenses including hire paid under the charter for time lost in the salvage, also repairs of damage and fuel oil consumed. The Charterers shall be bound by all measures taken by the Owners in order to secure payment of salvage and to fix its amount.

19. Sublet
The Charterers shall have the option of subletting the Vessel, giving due notice to the Owners, but the original Charterers shall always remain responsible to the Owners for due performance of the Charter.

20. War ("Conwartime 1993")
(A) For the purpose of this Clause, the words:
(i) "Owners" shall include the shipowners, bareboat charterers, disponent owners, managers or other operators who are charged with the management of the Vessel, and the Master; and
(ii) "War Risks" shall include any war (whether actual or threatened), act of war, civil war, hostilities, revolution, rebellion, civil commotion, warlike operations, the laying of mines (whether actual or reported), acts of piracy, acts of terrorists, acts of hostility or malicious damage, blockades (whether imposed against all vessels or imposed selectively against vessels of certain flags or ownership, or against certain cargoes or crews or otherwise howsoever), by any person, body, terrorist or political group, or the Government of any state whatsoever, which, in the reasonable judgement of the Master and/or the Owners, may be dangerous or are likely to be or to become dangerous to the Vessel, her cargo, crew or other persons on board the Vessel.
(B) The Vessel, unless the written consent of the Owners be first obtained, shall not be ordered to or required to continue to or through, any port, place, area or zone (whether of land or sea), or any waterway or canal, where

PART II
"BALTIME 1939" Uniform Time-Charter (as revised 2001)

it appears that the Vessel, her cargo, crew or other persons on board the Vessel, in the reasonable judgement of the Master and/or the Owners, may be, or are likely to be, exposed to War Risks. Should the Vessel be within any such place as aforesaid, which only becomes dangerous, or is likely to be or to become dangerous, after her entry into it, she shall be at liberty to leave it.

(C) The Vessel shall not be required to load contraband cargo, or to pass through any blockade, whether such blockade be imposed on all vessels, or is imposed selectively in any way whatsoever against vessels of certain flags or ownership, or against certain cargoes or crews or otherwise howsoever, or to proceed to an area where she shall be subject, or is likely to be subject to a belligerent's right of search and/or confiscation.

(D) (i) The Owners may effect war risks insurance in respect of the Hull and Machinery of the Vessel and their other interests (including, but not limited to, loss of earnings and detention, the crew and their Protection and Indemnity Risks), and the premiums and/or calls therefor shall be for their account.

(ii) If the Underwriters of such insurance should require payment of premiums and/or calls because, pursuant to the Charterers' orders, the Vessel is within, or is due to enter and remain within, any area or areas which are specified by such Underwriters as being subject to additional premiums because of War Risks, then such premiums and/or calls shall be reimbursed by the Charterers to the Owners at the same time as the next payment of hire is due.

(E) If the Owners become liable under the terms of employment to pay to the crew any bonus or additional wages in respect of sailing into an area which is dangerous in the manner defined by the said terms, then such bonus or additional wages shall be reimbursed to the Owners by the Charterers at the same time as the next payment of hire is due.

(F) The Vessel shall have liberty:-
(i) to comply with all orders, directions, recommendations or advice as to departure, arrival, routes, sailing in convoy, ports of call, stoppages, destinations, discharge of cargo, delivery, or in any other way whatsoever, which are given by the Government of the Nation under whose flag the Vessel sails, or other Government to whose laws the Owners are subject, or any other Government, body or group whatsoever acting with the power to compel compliance with their orders or directions;

(ii) to comply with the order, directions or recommendations of any war risks underwriters who have the authority to give the same under the terms of the war risks insurance;

(iii) to comply with the terms of any resolution of the Security Council of the United Nations, any directives of the European Community, the effective orders of any other Supranational body which has the right to issue and give the same, and with national laws aimed at enforcing the same to which the Owners are subject, and to obey the orders and directions of those who are charged with their enforcement;

(iv) to divert and discharge at any other port any cargo or part thereof which may render the Vessel liable to confiscation as a contraband carrier;

(v) to divert and call at any other port to change the crew or any part thereof or other persons on board the Vessel when there is reason to believe that they may be subject to internment, imprisonment or other sanctions.

(G) If in accordance with their rights under the foregoing provisions of this Clause, the Owners shall refuse to proceed to the loading or discharging ports, or any one or more of them, they shall immediately inform the Charterers. No cargo shall be discharged at any alternative port without first giving the Charterers notice of the Owners' intention to do so and requesting them to nominate a safe port for such discharge. Failing such nomination by the Charterers within 48 hours of the receipt of such notice and request, the Owners may discharge the cargo at any safe port of their own choice.

(H) If in compliance with any of the provisions of sub-clauses (B) to (G) of this Clause anything is done or not done, such shall not be deemed a deviation, but shall be considered as due fulfilment of this Charter.

21. Cancelling

Should the Vessel not be delivered by the date indicated in Box 22, the Charterers shall have the option of cancelling. If the Vessel cannot be delivered by the cancelling date, the Charterers, if required, shall declare within 48 hours after receiving notice thereof whether they cancel or will take delivery of the Vessel.

22. Dispute Resolution

*) **(A)** This Charter shall be governed by and construed in accordance with English law and any dispute arising out of or in connection with this Charter shall be referred to arbitration in London in accordance with the Arbitration Act 1996 or any statutory modification or re-enactment thereof save to the extent necessary to give effect to the provisions of this Clause.

The arbitration shall be conducted in accordance with the London Maritime Arbitrators Association (LMAA) Terms current at the time when the arbitration proceedings are commenced.

The reference shall be to three arbitrators. A party wishing to refer a dispute to arbitration shall appoint its arbitrator and send notice of such appointment in writing to the other party requiring the other party to appoint its own arbitrator within 14 calendar days of that notice and stating that it will appoint its arbitrator as sole arbitrator unless the other party appoints its own arbitrator and gives notice that it has done so within the 14 days specified. If the other party does not appoint its own arbitrator and give notice that it has done so within the 14 days specified, the party referring a dispute to arbitration may, without the requirement of any further prior notice to the other party, appoint its arbitrator as sole arbitrator and shall advise the other party accordingly. The award of a sole arbitrator shall be binding on both parties as if he had been appointed by agreement.

Nothing herein shall prevent the parties agreeing in writing to vary these provisions to provide for the appointment of a sole arbitrator.

In cases where neither the claim nor any counterclaim exceeds the sum of US$50,000 (or such other sum as the parties may agree) the arbitration shall be conducted in accordance with the LMAA Small Claims Procedure current at the time when the arbitration proceedings are commenced.

*) **(B)** This Charter shall be governed by and construed in accordance with Title 9 of the United States Code and the Maritime Law of the United States and any dispute arising out of or in connection with this Contract shall be referred to three persons at New York, one to be appointed by each of the parties hereto, and the third by the two so chosen; their decision or that of any two of them shall be final, and for the purposes of enforcing any award, judgement may be entered on an award by any court of competent jurisdiction. The proceedings shall be conducted in accordance with the rules of the Society of Maritime Arbitrators, Inc.

PART II
"BALTIME 1939" Uniform Time-Charter (as revised 2001)

In cases where neither the claim nor any counterclaim exceeds the sum of US$50,000 (or such other sum as the parties may agree) the arbitration shall be conducted in accordance with the Shortened Arbitration Procedure of the Society of Maritime Arbitrators, Inc. current at the time when the arbitration proceedings are commenced.

*) **(C)** This Charter shall be governed by and construed in accordance with the laws of the place mutually agreed by the parties and any dispute arising out of or in connection with this Charter shall be referred to arbitration at a mutually agreed place, subject to the procedures applicable there.

(D) Notwithstanding (A), (B) or (C) above, the parties may agree at any time to refer to mediation any difference and/or dispute arising out of or in connection with this Charter.

In the case of a dispute in respect of which arbitration has been commenced under (A), (B) or (C) above, the following shall apply:-

(i) Either party may at any time and from time to time elect to refer the dispute or part of the dispute to mediation by service on the other party of a written notice (the "Mediation Notice") calling on the other party to agree to mediation.

(ii) The other party shall thereupon within 14 calendar days of receipt of the Mediation Notice confirm that they agree to mediation, in which case the parties shall thereafter agree a mediator within a further 14 calendar days, failing which on the application of either party a mediator will be appointed promptly by the Arbitration Tribunal ("the Tribunal") or such person as the Tribunal may designate for that purpose. The mediation shall be conducted in such place and in accordance with such procedure and on such terms as the parties may agree or, in the event of disagreement, as may be set by the mediator.

(iii) If the other party does not agree to mediate, that fact may be brought to the attention of the Tribunal and may be taken into account by the Tribunal when allocating the costs of the arbitration as between the parties.

(iv) The mediation shall not affect the right of either party to seek such relief or take such steps as it considers necessary to protect its interest.

(v) Either party may advise the Tribunal that they have agreed to mediation. The arbitration procedure shall continue during the conduct of the mediation but the Tribunal may take the mediation timetable into account when setting the timetable for steps in the arbitration.

(vi) Unless otherwise agreed or specified in the mediation terms, each party shall bear its own costs incurred in the mediation and the parties shall share equally the mediator's costs and expenses.

(vii) The mediation process shall be without prejudice and confidential and no information or documents disclosed during it shall be revealed to the Tribunal except to the extent that they are disclosable under the law and procedure governing the arbitration.

(Note: The parties should be aware that the mediation process may not necessarily interrupt time limits.)

(E) If Box 23 in Part I is not appropriately filled in, sub-clause (A) of this Clause shall apply. Sub-clause (D) shall apply in all cases.

*) *(A), (B) and (C) are alternatives; indicate alternative agreed in Box 23.*

23. General Average
General Average shall be settled according to York/Antwerp Rules, 1994 and any subsequent modification thereof. Hire shall not contribute to General Average.

24. Commission
The Owners shall pay a commission at the rate stated in Box 24 to the party mentioned in Box 24 on any hire paid under the Charter, but in no case less than is necessary to cover the actual expenses of the Brokers and a reasonable fee for their work. If the full hire is not paid owing to breach of Charter by either of the parties the party liable therefor shall indemnify the Brokers against their loss of commission. Should the parties agree to cancel the Charter, the Owners shall indemnify the Brokers against any loss of commission but in such case the commission not to exceed the brokerage on one year's hire.

2. *Bill of Lading* (Conocimiento de Embarque)

Documento que acredita la recepción de la mercancía a bordo del buque porteador, dando cuenta de la cantidad y condiciones de la carga. Aunque no es un contrato, actúa como recibo de la carga, indicando su titularidad y las condiciones de transporte de la misma.

El Conocimiento de Embarque, como documento, cumple las siguientes funciones:

- Recibo de la carga, firmado por el capitán o por los agentes portuarios del armador en representación del fletador, que muestra la cantidad y condiciones de la carga. Se incluye el nombre del fletador, el consignatario, el puerto de carga, el destino y el nombre del buque; también se puede incluir el pago del flete.
- Titularidad de la carga, indicando que la propiedad de dicha carga puede ser transferida a otro.
- Un contrato (o evidencia de un contrato). En caso de no existir otro contrato este documento incluirá las condiciones del transporte. De existir un Contrato de Fletamento, se detallarán las condiciones, especificando que los términos del contrato están incluidos en el Conocimiento de Embarque.

Una vez cargadas las mercancías, el transportista ha de exigir al cargador los correspondientes contratos provisionales o *Mate's receipt* que serán canjeados por los *Bills of Lading* correspondientes.

MODELO DE *MATE'S RECEIPT*

Mates Receipt No.
Custom House Pass No.   Dated   Received on Board the M/V
Shipper   Consignee
From   To

Subject to all exemptions, terms and conditions in the Bill of Lading to be granted for these goods

Marks	No.	Description	Remarks

MODELO DE RECIBO DEL PILOTO

Recibo del piloto Nº.
Pasaporte Aduanas   Fechado   Recibido a Bordo del Buque
Armador   Consignatario
De   A

Sujeto a todas las exenciones, términos y condiciones del Conocimiento de Embarque como garantía de estos bienes

Referencia	Nº	Descripción	Observaciones

Seguidamente se incluye un modelo de la *Bill of Lading "Conlinebill 2000"*.

Page 1

Shipper (full style and address)	**LINER BILL OF LADING "CONLINEBILL 2000"**		
	Amended January 1950; August 1952; January 1973; July 1974; August 1976; January 1978; November 2000.		
Consignee (full style and address) or Order	B/L No.		Reference No.
	Vessel		
Notify Party (full style and address)	Port of loading		
	Port of discharge		

PARTICULARS DECLARED BY THE SHIPPER BUT NOT ACKNOWLEDGED BY THE CARRIER			
Container No./Seal No./Marks and Numbers	Number and kind of packages; description of cargo	Gross weight, kg	Measurement, m^3

SHIPPED on board in apparent good order and condition (unless otherwise stated herein) the total number of Containers/Packages or Units indicated in the Box opposite entitled "Total number of Containers/Packages or Units received by the Carrier" and the cargo as specified above, weight, measure, marks, numbers, quality, contents and value unknown, for carriage to the Port of discharge or so near thereunto as the vessel may safely get and lie always afloat, to be delivered in the like good order and condition at the Port of discharge unto the lawful holder of the Bill of Lading, on payment of freight as indicated to the right plus other charges incurred in accordance with the provisions contained in this Bill of Lading. In accepting this Bill of Lading the Merchant* expressly accepts and agrees to all its stipulations on both Page 1 and Page 2, whether written, printed, stamped or otherwise incorporated, as fully as if they were all signed by the Merchant. One original Bill of Lading must be surrendered duly endorsed in exchange for the cargo or delivery order, whereupon all other Bills of Lading to be void. IN WITNESS whereof the Carrier, Master or their Agent has signed the number of original Bills of Lading stated below right, all of this tenor and date.	Total number of Containers/Packages or Units received by the Carrier	
	Shipper's declared value	Declared value charge
	Freight details and charges	
Carrier's name/principal place of business	Date shipped on board	Place and date of issue
	Number of original Bills of Lading	
	Pre-carriage by**	
Signature .... Carrier or, for the Carrier .... as Master (Master's name/signature) .... as Agents (Agent's name/signature)	Place of receipt by pre-carrier**	
	Place of delivery by on-carrier**	

*As defined hereinafter (Cl. 1)
**Applicable only when pre-/on-carriage is arranged in accordance with Clause 8

LINER BILL OF LADING

Code Name: "CONLINEBILL 2000"

Page 2

1. Definition.
"Merchant" includes the shipper, the receiver, the consignor, the consignee, the holder of the Bill of Lading, the owner of the cargo and any person entitled to possession of the cargo.

2. Notification.
Any mention in this Bill of Lading of parties to be notified of the arrival of the cargo is solely for the information of the Carrier and failure to give such notification shall not involve the Carrier in any liability nor relieve the Merchant of any obligation hereunder.

3. Liability for Carriage Between Port of Loading and Port of Discharge.
(a) The International Convention for the Unification of Certain Rules of Law relating to Bills of Lading signed at Brussels on 25 August 1924 ("the Hague Rules") as amended by the Protocol signed at Brussels on 23 February 1968 ("the Hague-Visby Rules") and as enacted in the country of shipment shall apply to this Contract. When the Hague-Visby Rules are not enacted in the country of shipment, the corresponding legislation of the country of destination shall apply, irrespective of whether such legislation may only regulate outbound shipments.
When there is no enactment of the Hague-Visby Rules in either the country of shipment or in the country of destination, the Hague-Visby Rules shall apply to this Contract save where the Hague Rules as enacted in the country of shipment or, if no such enactment is in place, the Hague Rules as enacted in the country of destination apply compulsorily to this Contract.
The Protocol signed at Brussels on 21 December 1979 ("the SDR Protocol 1979") shall apply where the Hague-Visby Rules apply, whether mandatorily or by this Contract.
The Carrier shall in no case be responsible for loss of or damage to cargo arising prior to loading, after discharging, or with respect to deck cargo and live animals.
(b) If the Carrier is held liable in respect of delay, consequential loss or damage other than loss of or damage to the cargo, the liability of the Carrier shall be limited to the freight for the carriage covered by this Bill of Lading, or to the limitation amount as determined in sub-clause 3(a), whichever is the lesser.
(c) The aggregate liability of the Carrier and/or any of his servants, agents or independent contractors under this Contract shall, in no circumstances, exceed the limits of liability for the total loss of the cargo under sub-clause 3(a) or, if applicable, the Additional Clause.

4. Law and Jurisdiction.
Disputes arising out of or in connection with this Bill of Lading shall be exclusively determined by the courts and in accordance with the law of the place where the Carrier has his principal place of business, as stated on Page 1, except as provided elsewhere herein.

5. The Scope of Carriage.
The intended carriage shall not be limited to the direct route but shall be deemed to include any proceeding or returning to or stopping or slowing down at or off any ports or places for any reasonable purpose connected with the carriage including bunkering, loading, discharging, or other cargo operations and maintenance of Vessel and crew.

6. Substitution of Vessel.
The Carrier shall be at liberty to carry the cargo or part thereof to the Port of discharge by the said or other vessel or vessels either belonging to the Carrier or others, or by other means of transport, proceeding either directly or indirectly to such port.

7. Transhipment.
The Carrier shall be at liberty to tranship, lighter, land and store the cargo either on shore or afloat and reship and forward the same to the Port of discharge.

8. Liability for Pre- and On-Carriage.
When the Carrier arranges pre-carriage of the cargo from a place other than the Vessel's Port of loading or on-carriage of the cargo to a place other than the Vessel's Port of discharge, the Carrier shall contract as the Merchant's Agent only and the Carrier shall not be liable for any loss or damage arising during any part of the carriage other than between the Port of loading and the Port of discharge even though the freight for the whole carriage has been collected by him.

9. Loading and Discharging.
(a) Loading and discharging of the cargo shall be arranged by the Carrier or his Agent.
(b) The Merchant shall, at his risk and expense, handle and/or store the cargo before loading and after discharging.
(c) Loading and discharging may commence without prior notice.
(d) The Merchant or his Agent shall tender the cargo when the Vessel is ready to load and as fast as the Vessel can receive including, if required by the Carrier, outside ordinary working hours notwithstanding any custom of the port. If the Merchant or his Agent fails to tender the cargo when the Vessel is ready to load or fails to load as fast as the Vessel can receive the cargo, the Carrier shall be relieved of any obligation to load such cargo, the Vessel shall be entitled to leave the port without further notice and the Merchant shall be liable to the Carrier for deadfreight and/or any overtime charges, losses, costs and expenses incurred by the Carrier.
(e) The Merchant or his Agent shall take delivery of the cargo as fast as the Vessel can discharge including, if required by the Carrier, outside ordinary working hours notwithstanding any custom of the port. If the Merchant or his Agent fails to take delivery of the cargo the Carrier's discharging of the cargo shall be deemed fulfilment of the contract of carriage. Should the cargo not be applied for within a reasonable time, the Carrier may sell the same privately or by auction. If the Merchant or his Agent fails to take delivery of the cargo as fast as the Vessel can discharge, the Merchant shall be liable to the Carrier for any overtime charges, losses, costs and expenses incurred by the Carrier.
(f) The Merchant shall accept his reasonable proportion of unidentified loose cargo.

10. Freight, Charges, Costs, Expenses, Duties, Taxes and Fines.
(a) Freight, whether paid or not, shall be considered as fully earned upon loading and non-returnable in any event. Unless otherwise specified, freight and/or charges under this Contract are payable by the Merchant to the Carrier on demand. Interest at Libor (or its successor) plus 2 per cent. shall run from fourteen days after the date when freight and charges are payable.
(b) The Merchant shall be liable for all costs and expenses of fumigation, gathering and sorting loose cargo and weighing onboard, repairing damage to and replacing packing due to excepted causes, and any extra handling of the cargo for any of the aforementioned reasons.
(c) The Merchant shall be liable for any dues, duties, taxes and charges which under any denomination may be levied, *inter alia*, on the basis of freight, weight of cargo or tonnage of the Vessel.
(d) The Merchant shall be liable for all fines, penalties, costs, expenses and losses which the Carrier, Vessel or cargo may incur through non-observance of Customs House and/or import or export regulations.
(e) The Carrier is entitled in case of incorrect declaration of contents, weights, measurements or value of the cargo to claim double the amount of freight which would have been due if such declaration had been correctly given. For the purpose of ascertaining the actual facts, the Carrier shall have the right to obtain from the Merchant the original invoice and to have the cargo inspected and its contents, weight, measurement or value verified.

11. Lien.
The Carrier shall have a lien on all cargo for any amount due under this contract and the costs of recovering the same and shall be entitled to sell the cargo privately or by auction to satisfy any such claims.

12. General Average and Salvage.
General Average shall be adjusted, stated and settled in London according to the York-Antwerp Rules 1994, or any modification thereof, in respect of all cargo, whether carried on or under deck. In the event of accident, danger, damage or disaster before or after commencement of the voyage resulting from any cause whatsoever, whether due to negligence or not, for which or for the consequence of which the Carrier is not responsible by statute, contract or otherwise, the Merchant shall contribute with the Carrier in General Average to the payment of any sacrifice, losses or expenses of a General Average nature that may be made or incurred, and shall pay salvage and special charges incurred in respect of the cargo. If a salving vessel is owned or operated by the Carrier, salvage shall be paid for as fully as if the salving vessel or vessels belonged to strangers.

13. Both-to-Blame Collision Clause.
If the Vessel comes into collision with another vessel as a result of the negligence of the other vessel and any act, negligence or default of the Master, Mariner, Pilot or the servants of the Carrier in the navigation or in the management of the Vessel, the Merchant will indemnify the Carrier against all loss or liability to the other or non-carrying vessel or her Owner in so far as such loss or liability represents loss of or damage to or any claim whatsoever of the owner of the cargo paid or payable by the other or non-carrying vessel or her Owner to the owner of the cargo and set-off, recouped or recovered by the other or non-carrying vessel or her Owner as part of his claim against the carrying vessel or Carrier. The foregoing provisions shall also apply where the Owner, operator or those in charge of any vessel or vessels or objects other than, or in addition to, the colliding vessels or objects are at fault in respect of a collision or contact.

14. Government directions, War, Epidemics, Ice, Strikes, etc.
(a) The Master and the Carrier shall have liberty to comply with any order or directions or recommendations in connection with the carriage under this Contract given by any Government or Authority, or anybody acting or purporting to act on behalf of such Government or Authority, or having under the terms of the insurance on the Vessel the right to give such orders or directions or recommendations.
(b) Should it appear that the performance of the carriage would expose the Vessel or any cargo onboard to risk of seizure, damage or delay, in consequence of war, warlike operations, blockade, riots, civil commotions or piracy, or any person onboard to risk of loss of life or freedom, or that any such risk has increased, the Master may discharge the cargo at the Port of loading or any other safe and convenient port.
(c) Should it appear that epidemics; quarantine; ice; labour troubles, labour obstructions, strikes, lockouts (whether onboard or on shore); difficulties in loading or discharging would prevent the Vessel from leaving the Port of loading or reaching or entering the Port of discharge or there discharging in the usual manner and departing therefrom, all of which safely and without unreasonable delay, the Master may discharge the cargo at the Port of loading or any other safe and convenient port.
(d) The discharge, under the provisions of this Clause, of any cargo shall be deemed due fulfilment of the contract of carriage.
(e) If in connection with the exercise of any liberty under this Clause any extra expenses are incurred they shall be paid by the Merchant in addition to the freight, together with return freight, if any, and a reasonable compensation for any extra services rendered to the cargo.

15. Defences and Limits of Liability for the Carrier, Servants and Agents.
(a) It is hereby expressly agreed that no servant or agent of the Carrier (which for the purpose of this Clause includes every independent contractor from time to time employed by the Carrier) shall in any circumstances whatsoever be under any liability whatsoever to the Merchant under this Contract of carriage for any loss, damage or delay of whatsoever kind arising or resulting directly or indirectly from any act, neglect or default on his part while acting in the course of or in connection with his employment.
(b) Without prejudice to the generality of the foregoing provisions in this Clause, every exemption from liability, limitation, condition and liberty herein contained and every right, defence and immunity of whatsoever nature applicable to the Carrier or to which the Carrier is entitled, shall also be available and shall extend to protect every such servant and agent of the Carrier acting as aforesaid.
(c) The Merchant undertakes that no claim shall be made against any servant or agent of the Carrier and, if any claim should nevertheless be made, to indemnify the Carrier against all consequences thereof.
(d) For the purpose of all the foregoing provisions of this Clause the Carrier is or shall be deemed to be acting as agent or trustee on behalf of and for the benefit of all persons who might be his servants or agents from time to time and all such persons shall to this extent be or be deemed to be parties to this Contract of carriage.

16. Stowage.
(a) The Carrier shall have the right to stow cargo by means of containers, trailers, transportable tanks, flats, pallets, or similar articles of transport used to consolidate goods.
(b) The Carrier shall have the right to carry containers, trailers, transportable tanks and covered flats, whether stowed by the Carrier or received by him in a stowed condition from the Merchant, on or under deck without notice to the Merchant.

17. Shipper-Packed Containers, trailers, transportable tanks, flats and pallets.
(a) If a container has not been filled, packed or stowed by the Carrier, the Carrier shall not be liable for any loss of or damage to its contents and the Merchant shall cover any loss or expense incurred by the Carrier, if such loss, damage or expense has been caused by:
(i) negligent filling, packing or stowing of the container;
(ii) the contents being unsuitable for carriage in container; or
(iii) the unsuitability or defective condition of the container unless the container has been supplied by the Carrier and the unsuitability or defective condition would not have been apparent upon reasonable inspection at or prior to the time when the container was filled, packed or stowed.
(b) The provisions of sub-clause (i) of this Clause also apply with respect to trailers, transportable tanks, flats and pallets which have not been filled, packed or stowed by the Carrier.
(c) The Carrier does not accept liability for damage due to the unsuitability or defective condition of reefer equipment or trailers supplied by the Merchant.

18. Return of Containers.
(a) Containers, pallets or similar articles of transport supplied by or on behalf of the Carrier shall be returned to the Carrier in the same order and condition as handed over to the Merchant, normal wear and tear excepted, with interiors clean and within the time prescribed in the Carrier's tariff or elsewhere.
(b) The Merchant shall be liable to the Carrier for any loss, damage to, or delay, including demurrage and detention incurred by or sustained to containers, pallets or similar articles of transport during the period between handing over to the Merchant and return to the Carrier.

ADDITIONAL CLAUSE

U.S. Trade. Period of Responsibility.
(i) In case the Contract evidenced by this Bill of Lading is subject to the Carriage of Goods by Sea Act of the United States of America, 1936 (U.S. COGSA), then the provisions stated in said Act shall govern before loading and after discharge and throughout the entire time the cargo is in the Carrier's custody and in which event freight shall be payable on the cargo coming into the Carrier's custody.
(ii) If the U.S. COGSA applies, and unless the nature and value of the cargo has been declared by the shipper before the cargo has been handed over to the Carrier and inserted in this Bill of Lading, the Carrier shall in no event be or become liable for any loss or damage to the cargo in an amount exceeding USD 500 per package or customary freight unit.

El ejemplo anterior es un formulario tipo de Conocimiento de Embarque; no obstante, existen distintos tipos de Conocimiento de Embarque, clasificados por las condiciones establecidas en sus respectivas cláusulas.

CLEAN B/L	DIRTY/FOUL B/L
SHORT FORM B/L	LONG FORM B/L
RECEIVED B/L	ON BOARD B/L
STRAIGHT B/L	ORDER B/L

Versus

C/E LIMPIO, NETO	C/E CON RESERVAS/SUCIO
C/E ABREVIADO	C/E DETALLADO
C/E RECIBIDO PARA EMBARQUE	C/E A BORDO
C/E NEGOCIABLE	C/E NO NEGOCIABLE

Versus

a. *Clean B/L*: No contiene ninguna cláusula que indique defectos en la carga
b. *Foul B/L*: Contiene cláusulas con respecto a la carga, bien porque el embalaje de dicha carga es defectuoso y el fletador no se responsabiliza de los riesgos que pueda sufrir la carga, bien porque existen objeciones por parte del fletador en cuanto al contenido, peso, calidad o especificación de la mercancía transportada.
c. *Received for Shipment B/L*: El fletador confía la custodia de la mercancía al armador o consignatario antes de que el barco llegue a puerto para la carga o esté preparado para cargar la mercancía. También denominada *"Custody B/L".*
d. *On board B/L*: La mercancía ya ha sido cargada.
e. *Straight B/L*: Término utilizado en EEUU para una Bill of Lading emitida exclusivamente a favor de un consignatario. Este documento rara vez es emitido, excepto para mercancías de gran valor.

f. *Order B/L*: La gran mayoría de los actuales Conocimientos de Embarque se corresponden con este tipo y son negociables. La titularidad de los bienes se transmite a una compañía o a un agente designado por ésta; normalmente se indica en el reverso del documento a quien se transfiere dicha titularidad.

Otros tipos de Conocimientos de Embarque menos habituales son:

a. *Blank B/L*: Conocimiento de embarque en blanco
b. *Direct B/L*: Sólo cubre el transporte de la mercancía de puerto a puerto.
c. *Homeward B/L*: Conocimiento de retorno
d. *House B/L*: Conocimiento de embarque interno (Hijo)
e. *Liner B/L*: Expedida por el armador o fletador de un buque de carga general, sin que se incluya en el transporte ningún tipo de Contrato de Fletamento por parte del armador o del consignatario.
f. *Master B/L*: Conocimiento de embarque principal (Madre)
g. *Named B/L*: Conocimiento de embarque nominativo
h. *Open B/L*: No indica el destinatario de la mercancía. El titular de la mercancía tendría derecho a realizar la entrega de la mercancía, pero no podría conservar la titularidad si el propietario así lo indica en un momento determinado del transporte.
i. *Stale B/L*: Conocimiento de embarque vencido o fuera de plazo.
j. *Through B/L*: Para mercancía transportada en parte por mar, en parte por tierra, o cuando se realiza un traspaso de la mercancía de un buque a otro en puertos intermedios.

La evolución en el transporte de mercancías ha originado una nueva filosofía en este campo, la intermodalidad, que pasa del concepto *port to port* (puerto-puerto) al concepto *door to door* (puerta-puerta). Este cambio implica la utilización de diferentes modos de transporte (marítimo, ferroviario, terrestre, aéreo, fluvial, etc) lo que demanda nuevos documentos tipo. Como ejemplo se reproduce a continuación la así denominada *"Combined Transport Bill of Lading"*

Code Name: "COMBICONBILL"			B/L No.
Shipper			
			Reference No.
		Negotiable	
		COMBINED TRANSPORT BILL OF LADING	
		Revised 1995	
Consigned to order of			
Notify party/address			
	Place of receipt		
Ocean Vessel	Port of loading		
Port of discharge	Place of delivery	Freight payable at	Number of original Bills of Lading
Marks and Nos.	Quantity and description of goods		Gross weight, kg, Measurement, m³

Particulars above declared by Shipper

Freight and charges	RECEIVED the goods in apparent good order and condition and, as far as ascertained by reasonable means of checking, as specified above unless otherwise stated. The Carrier, in accordance with and to the extent of the provisions contained in this Bill of Lading, and with liberty to sub-contract, undertakes to perform and/or in his own name to procure performance of the combined transport and the delivery of the goods, including all services related thereto, from the place and time of taking the goods in charge to the place and time of delivery and accepts responsibility for such transport and such services. One of the Bills of Lading must be surrendered duly endorsed in exchange for the goods or delivery order. IN WITNESS whereof TWO (2) original Bills of Lading have been signed, if not otherwise stated above, one of which being accomplished the other(s) to be void.
Shipper's declared value of ...... subject to payment of above extra charge. **Note:** The Merchant's attention is called to the fact that according to Clauses 10 to 12 and Clause 24 of this Bill of Lading, the liability of the Carrieris, in most cases, limited in respect of loss of or damage to the goods and delay.	Place and date of issue Signed for .... as Carrier by .... As agent(s) only to the Carrier

p.t.o.

COMBINED TRANSPORT BILL OF LADING

Adopted by The Baltic and International Maritime Council in January, 1971 (as revised 1995)

Code Name: "COMBICONBILL"

I. GENERAL PROVISIONS

1. **Applicability.**

Notwithstanding the heading "Combined Transport", the provisions set out and referred to in this Bill of Lading shall also apply, if the transport as described in this Bill of Lading is performed by one mode of transport only.

2. **Definitions**.

"Carrier" means the party on whose behalf this Bill of Lading has been signed.

"Merchant" includes the Shipper, the Receiver, the Consignor, the Consignee, the holder of this Bill of Lading and the owner of the goods.

3. **Carrier's Tariff.**

The terms of the Carrier's applicable Tariff at the date of shipment are incorporated herein. Copies of the relevant provisions of the applicable Tariff are available from the Carrier upon request. In the case of inconsistency between this Bill of Lading and the applicable Tariff, this Bill of Lading shall prevail.

4. **Time Bar.**

All liability whatsoever of the Carrier shall cease unless suit is brought within 9 months after delivery of the goods or the date when the goods should have been delivered.

5. **Law and Jurisdiction.**

Disputes arising under this Bill of Ladinq shall be determined by the courts and in accordance with the law at the place where the Carrier has his principal place of business.

II. PERFORMANCE OF THE CONTRACT

6. **Methods and Routes of Transportation.**

(1) The Carrier is entitled to perform the transport and all services related thereto in any reasonable manner and by any reasonable means, methods and routes.

(2) In accordance herewith, for instance, in the event of carriage by sea, vessels may sail with or without pilots, undergo repairs, adjust equipment, drydock and tow vessels in all situations.

7. **Optional Stowage.**

(1) Goods may be stowed by the Carrier by means of containers, trailers, transportable tanks, flats, pallets, or similar articles of transport used to consolidate goods.

(2) Containers, trailers, transportable tanks and covered flats, whether stowed by the Carrier or received by him in a stowed condition from the Merchant, may be carried on or under deck without notice to the Merchant.

8. **Hindrances etc. Affecting Performance.**

(1) The Carrier shall use reasonable endeavours to complete the transport and to deliver the goods at the place designated for delivery.

(2) If at any time the performance of the contract as evidenced by this Bill of Lading is or will be affected by any hindrance, risk, delay, difficulty or disadvantage of whatsoever kind, and if by virtue of sub-clause 8 (1) the Carrier has no duty to complete the performance of the contract, the Carrier (whether or not the transport is commenced) may elect to:

(a) treat the performance of this Contract as terminated and place the goods at the Merchant's disposal at any place which the Carrier shall deem safe and convenient;

or

(b) deliver the goods at the place designated for delivery.

(3) If the goods are not taken delivery of by the Merchant within a reasonable time after the Carrier has called upon him to take delivery, the Carrier shall be at liberty to put the goods in safe custody on behalf of the Merchant at the latter's risk and expense.

(4) In any event the Carrier shall be entitled to full freight for goods received for transportation and additional compensation for extra costs resulting from the circumstances referred to above.

III. CARRIER'S LIABILITY

9. **Basic Liability.**

(1) The Carrier shall be liable for loss of or damage to the goods occurring between the time when he receives the goods into his charge and the time of delivery.

(2) The Carrier shall be responsible for the acts and omissions of any person of whose services he makes use for the performance of the contract of carriage evidenced by this Bill of Lading.

(3) The Carrier shall, however, be relieved of liability for any loss or damage if such loss or damage arose or resulted from:

(a) The wrongful act or neglect of the Merchant.

(b) Compliance with the Instructions of the person entitled to give them.

(c) The lack of, or defective conditions of packing in the case of goods which, by their nature, are liable to wastage or to be damaged when not packed or when not properly packed.

(d) Handling, loading, stowage or unloading of the goods by or on behalf of the Merchant.

(e) Inherent vice of the goods.

(f) Insufficiency or inadequacy of marks or numbers on the goods, covering, or unit loads.

(g) Strikes or lock-outs or stoppages or restraints of labour from whatever cause whether partial or general.

(h) Any cause or event which the Carrier could not avoid and the consequence whereof he could not prevent by the exercise of reasonable diligence.

(4) Where under sub-clause 9 (3) the Carrier is not under any liability in respect of some of the factors causing the loss or damage, he shall only be liable to the extent that those factors for which he is liable under this Clause have contributed to the loss or damage.

(5) The burden of proving that the loss or damage was due to one or more of the causes or events, specified in (a), (b) and (h) of sub-clause 9 (3) shall rest upon the Carrier.

(6) When the Carrier establishes that in the circumstances of the case, the loss or damage could be attributed to one or more of the causes or events, specified in (c) to (g) of sub-clause 9 (3), it shall be presumed that it was so caused. The Merchant shall, however, be entitled to prove that the loss or damage was not, in fact, caused either wholly or partly by one or more of the causes or events.

10. **Amount of Compensation.**

(1) When the Carrier is liable for compensation in respect of loss of or damage to the goods, such compensation shall be calculated by reference to the value of such goods at the place and time they are delivered to the Merchant in accordance with the contract or should have been so delivered.

(2) The value of the goods shall be fixed according to the commodity exchange price or, if there be no such price, according to the current market price or, if there be no commodity exchange price or current market price, by reference to the normal value of goods of the same kind and quality.

(3) Compensation shall not, however, exceed two Special Drawing Rights per kilogramme of gross weight of the goods lost or damaged.

(4) Higher compensation may be claimed only when, with the consent of the Carrier, the value for the goods declared by the Shipper which exceeds the limits laid down in this Clause has been stated on the face of this Bill of Lading at the place indicated. In that case the amount of the declared value shall be substituted for that limit.

11. **Special Provisions for Liability and Compensation.**

(1) Notwithstanding anything provided for in Clauses 9 and 10 of this Bill of Lading, if it can be proved where the loss or damage occurred, the Carrier and the Merchant shall, as to the liability of the Carrier, be entitled to require such liability to be determined by the provisions contained in any international convention or national law, which provisions:

(a) cannot be departed from by private contract, to the detriment of the claimant, and

(b) would have applied if the Merchant had made a separate and direct contract with the Carrier in respect of the particular stage of transport where the loss or damage occurred and received as evidence thereof any particular document which must be issued if such international convention or national law shall apply.

(2) Insofar as there is no mandatory law applying to carriage by sea by virtue of the provisions of sub-clause 11 (1), the liability of the Carrier in respect of any carriage by sea shall be determined by the International Brussels Convention 1924 as amended by the Protocol signed at Brussels on February 23rd 1968 - The Hague/Visby Rules.

The Hague/Visby Rules shall also determine the liability of the Carrier in respect of carriage by inland waterways as if such carriage were carriage by sea. Furthermore, they shall apply to all goods, whether carried on deck or under deck.

12. **Delay, Consequential Loss, etc.**

If the Carrier is held liable in respect of delay, consequential loss or damage other than loss of or damage to the goods, the liability of the Carrier shall be limited to the freight for the transport covered by this Bill of Lading, or to the value of the goods as determined in Clause 10, whichever is the lesser.

13. **Notice of Loss of or Damage to the Goods.**

(1) Unless notice of loss of or damage to the goods, specifying the general nature of such loss or damage, is given in writing by the Merchant to the Carrier when the goods are handed over to the Merchant, such handing over is *prima facie* evidence of the Delivery by the Carrier of the goods as described in this Bill of Lading.

(2) Where the loss or damage is not apparent, the same *prima facie* effect shall apply if notice in writing is not given within three (3) consecutive days after the day when the goods were handed over to the Merchant.

14. **Defences and Limits for the Carrier, Servants, etc.**

(1) The defences and limits of liability provided for in this Bill of Lading shall apply in any action against the Carrier for loss or damage to the goods whether the action can be founded in contract or in tort.

(2) The Carrier shall not be entitled to the benefit of the limitation of liability provided for in sub-clause 10 (3), if it is proved that the loss or damage resulted from a personal act or omission of the Carrier done with intent to cause such loss or damage or recklessly and with knowledge that damage would probably result.

(3) The Merchant undertakes that no claim shall be made against any servant, agent or other persons whose services the Carrier has used In order to perform this Contract and if any claim should nevertheless be made, to indemnify the Carrier against all consequences thereof.

(4) However, the provisions of this Bill of Lading apply whenever claims relating to the performance of this Contract are made against any servant, agent or other person whose services the Carrier has used in order to perform this Contract, whether such claims are founded in contract or in tort. In entering into this Contract, the Carrier, to the extent of such provisions, does so not only on his own behalf but also as agent or trustee for such persons. The aggregate liability of the Carrier and such persons shall not exceed the limits in Clauses 10, 11 and 24, respectively.

IV. DESCRIPTION OF GOODS

15. **Carrier's Responsibility.**

The information in this Bill of Lading shall be *prima facie* evidence of the taking in charge by the Carrier of the goods as described by such information unless a contrary indication, such as "shipper's weight, load and count", "Shipper-packed container" or similar expressions, have been made in the printed text or superimposed on the Bill of Lading. Proof to the contrary shall not be admissible when the Bill of Lading has been transferred, or the equivalent electronic data interchange message has been transmitted to and acknowledged by the Consignee who in good faith has relied and acted thereon.

16. **Shipper's Responsibility.**

The Shipper shall be deemed to have guaranteed to the Carrier the accuracy, at the time the goods were taken in charge by the Carrier, of the description of the goods, marks, number, quantity and weight, as furnished by him, and the Shipper shall defend, indemnify and hold harmless the Carrier against all loss, damage and expenses arising or resulting from inaccuracies in or inadequacy of such particulars. The right of the Carrier to such indemnity shall in no way limit his responsibility and liability under this Bill of Lading to any person other than the Shipper. The Shipper shall remain liable even if the Bill of Lading has been transferred by him.

17. **Shipper-packed Containers, etc.**

(1) If a container has not been filled, packed or stowed by the Carrier, the Carrier shall not be liable for any loss of or damage to its contents and the Merchant shall cover any loss or expense incurred by the Carrier, if such loss, damage or expense has been caused by:

(a) negligent filling, packing or stowing of the container;

(b) the contents being unsuitable for carriage in container; or

(c) the unsuitability or defective condition of the container unless the container has been supplied by the Carrier and the unsuitability or defective condition would not have been apparent upon reasonable inspection at or prior to the time when the container was filled, packed or stowed.

(2) The provisions of sub-clause (1) of this Clause also apply with respect to trailers, transportable tanks, flats and pallets which have not been filled, packed or stowed by the Carrier.

(3) The Carrier does not accept liability for damage due to the unsuitability or defective condition of reefer equipment or trailers supplied by the Merchant.

18. **Dangerous Goods.**

(1) The Merchant shall comply with all internationally recognised requirements and all rules which apply according to national law or by reason of international Convention, relating to the carriage of goods of a dangerous nature, and shall in any event inform the Carrier in writing of the exact nature of the danger before goods of a dangerous nature are taken into charge by the Carrier and indicate to him, if need be, the precautions to be taken.

(2) Goods of a dangerous nature which the Carrier did not know were dangerous, may, at any time or place, be unloaded, destroyed, or rendered harmless, without compensation; further, the Merchant shall be liable for all expenses, loss or damage arising out of their handing over for carriage or of their carriage.

(3) If any goods shipped with the knowledge of the Carrier as to their dangerous nature shall become a danger to any person or property, they may in like manner be landed at any place or destroyed or rendered innocuous by the Carrier without liability on the part of the Carrier except to General Average, if any.

19. **Return of Containers.**

(1) For the purpose of this Clause the Consignor shall mean the Person who concludes this Contract with the Carrier and the Consignee shall mean the person entitled to receive the goods from the Carrier.

(2) Containers, pallets or similar articles of transport supplied by or on behalf of the Carrier shall be returned to the Carrier in the same order and condition as handed over to the Merchant, normal wear and tear excepted, with interiors clean and within the time prescribed in the Carrier's tariff or elsewhere.

(3)(a) The Consignor shall be liable for any loss of, damage to, or delay, including demurrage, of such articles, incurred during the period between handing over to the Consignor and return to the Carrier for carriage.

(b) The Consignor and the Consignee shall be jointly and severally liable for any lose of, damage to, or delay, including demurrage, of such articles, incurred during the period between handing over to the Consignee and return to the Carrier.

V. FREIGHT AND LIEN

20. **Freight.**

(1) Freight shall be deemed earned when the goods have been taken in charge by the Carrier and shall be paid in any event.

(2) The Merchant's attention is drawn to the stipulations concerning currency in which the freight and charges are to be paid, rate of exchange, devaluation and other contingencies relative to freight and charges in the relevant tariff conditions. If no such stipulation as to devaluation exists or is applicable the following shall apply:

If the currency in which freight and charges are quoted is devalued between the date of the freight agreement and the date when the freight and charges are paid, then all freight and charges shall be automatically and immediately increased in proportion to the extent of the devaluation of the said currency.

(3) For the purpose of verifying the freight basis, the Carrier reserves the right to have the contents of containers, trailers or similar articles of transport inspected in order to ascertain the weight, measurement, value, or nature of the goods.

21. **Lien.**

The Carrier shall have a lien on the goods for any amount due under this Contract and for the costs of recovering the same, and may enforce such lien in any reasonable manner, including sale or disposal of the goods.

VI. MISCELLANEOUS PROVISIONS

22. **General Average.**

(1) General Average shall be adjusted at any port or place at the Carrier's option, and to be settled according to the York-Antwerp Rules 1994, or any modification thereof, this covering all goods, whether carried on or under deck. The New Jason Clause as approved by BIMCO to be considered as incorporated herein.

(2) Such security including a cash deposit as the Carrier may deem sufficient to cover the estimated contribution of the qoods and any salvage and special charges thereon, shall, if required, be submitted to the Carrier prior to delivery of the goods.

23. **Both-to-Blame Collision Clause.**

The Both-to-Blame Collision Clause as adopted by BIMCO shall be considered incorporated herein.

24. **U.S. Trade.**

(1) In case the contract evidenced by this Bill of Lading is subject to the Carriage of Goods by Sea Act of the United States of America, 1936 (U.S. COGSA), then the provisions stated in the said Act shall govern before loading and after discharge and throughout the entire time the goods are in the Carrier's custody.

(2) If the U.S. COGSA applies, and unless the nature and value of the goods have been declared by the shipper before the goods have been handed over to the Carrier and inserted in this Bill of Lading, the Carrier shall in no event be or become liable for any loss of or damage to the goods in an amount exceeding USD 500 per package or customary freight unit.

3. Contrato de remolque

El contrato de remolque establece que el remolcador se compromete a colaborar en las maniobras de atraque y desatraque de otro buque a cambio de una remuneración, siempre que las circunstancias no entrañen riesgo o peligro.

Hasta la Segunda Guerra Mundial, las compañías dedicadas a prestar servicios de remolque a las naves obtenían su principal fuente de ingresos por la prestación de servicios de remolque portuario (*harbour towage*), pero, a partir de dicha fecha, dichas compañías comienzan a prestar también servicios de remolque de altura (*ocean towage*), con lo que las condiciones que se establecían en los contratos han de variar, ya que, aunque la mayoría son aplicables tanto al remolque maniobra como al remolque oceánico, otras no resultan adecuadas para la segunda modalidad.

Una vez descubierto el interés empresarial que supone el remolque de altura, aumenta la competencia entre las empresas dedicadas a ofrecer estos servicios, lo que provoca la aparición de formularios con distintas condiciones, a fin de captar clientes. Todos ello hace que se busque un modelo reconocido a nivel internacional que satisfaga tanto a los empresarios como a los usuarios.

Hoy en día existe un modelo de contrato aceptado por gran parte de los operadores, que se refleja en dos modelos, según las condiciones en que se pacta el remolque, las conocidas pólizas TOWCON y TOWHIRE. Ambos documentos son iguales en la forma, pero con variaciones en las condiciones de pago que se establecen; el TOWCON habla del término "*lump sum*" (a tanto alzado) por el que se negocia el precio del remolque por la totalidad del viaje, mientras que en la póliza TOWHIRE el precio se fija por cada día de alquiler del remolcador.

A continuación reproducimos los dos modelos de contratos de remolque más comunes.

1. Date and place of Agreement	RECOMMENDED INTERNATIONAL OCEAN TOWAGE AGREEMENT (L U M P S U M) CODE NAME: "TOWCON" PART I
2. Tugowner/place of business	3. Hirer/place of business
4. T o w (name and type)	5. Gross tonnage/displacement tonnage
6. Maximum length/maximum breadth & towing draught (fore and aft)	7. Flag and place of registry
8. Registered owners	9. Classification society
10. P. & I. liability insurers	11. General condition of tow
12. Particulars of cargo and/or ballast and/or other property on board the tow	
13. T u g (name and type)	14. Flag and place of registry
15. Gross tonnage	16. Classification society
17. P. & I. liability insurers	
18. Certificated bollard pull (if any)	19. Indicated horse power
20. Estimated daily average bunker oil consumption in good weather and smooth water	
(a) at full towing power with tow	
(b) at full sea speed without tow	
21. Winches and main towing gear	

(continued)

(continued)   **"TOWCON" INTERNATIONAL OCEAN TOWAGE AGREEMENT (LUMP SUM)**   PART I

22. Nature of service(s) (Cl. 1)		23. Contemplated route (Cl. 17)
24. Place of departure (Cl. 7)	25. Place of destination (Cl. 8)	
26. Free time at place of departure (Cl. 2(g))		27. Free time at place of destination (Cl. 2(g))

28. Notices (Place of departure) (Cl. 7(c))	29. Delay payment (Cl. 2(g))
(a) Initial departure period (from/to)	(a) Port rate
(b) Initial departure notice (days notice/days period)	(b) Sea rate
(c) Final departure period and notice (days notice/days period)	30. Riding crew to be provided by (also state number to be provided) (Cl. 9)
(d) Final departure time and date notice (days notice)	
(e) Notices to be given to	31. If riding crew provided by Tugowner state amount per man per day payable by Hirer (Cl. 9)

32. Lump sum towage price (also state when each instalment due and payable) (Cl. 2)	33. Payment of lump sum & other amounts (state currency, mode of payment, place of payment and bank account) (Cl. 2)
(a) Lump sum towage price	
(b) amount due and payable on signing agreement	
(c) amount due and payable on sailing of tug & tow from place of departure	
(d) amount due and payable on passing of tug and tow off	
(e) amount due and payable on arrival of tug & tow at place of destination	

34. Interest rate (%) per annum to run from (state number of days) after any sum is due (Cl. 5)	35. Security (state sum, by whom to be provided and when) (optional, only to be filled in if expressly agreed) (Cl. 6)
36. Current cost of tug's bunker oil (also state type of bunkers) (Cl. 2(e))	37. Cancelling date, if any agreed (Cl. 16(e))
38. Cancellation fee (Cl. 16)	39. Numbers of additional clauses, covering special provisions, if agreed

It is mutually agreed between the party mentioned in Box 2 (hereinafter called "the Tugowner") and the party mentioned in Box 3 (hereinafter called "the Hirer") that the Tugowner shall, subject to the terms and conditions of this Agreement which consists of PART I including additional clauses, if any agreed and stated in Box 39, and PART II, use his best endeavours to perform the towage or other service(s) as set out herein. In the event of a conflict of terms and conditions, the provisions of PART I and any additional clauses, if agreed, shall prevail over those of PART II to the extent of such conflict but no further.

Signature (Tugowner)	Signature (Hirer)

INSTRUCTIONS ON HOW TO FILL IN BOX 28 in PART I

Notices to be communicated according to clause 7(c)

Initial Departure Period (Box 28(a))
The Tow shall be ready to sail from the place of departure between the dates indicated.

Initial Departure Notice (Box 28 (b))
The Hirer shall give the Tugowner the number of days notice of the number of days period falling within the initial departure period as to when the Tow will be ready to depart.

Final Departure Period and Notice (Box 28 (c))
The Hirer shall give the Tugowner the number of days notice of the number of days period falling within the initial departure notice period as to when the Tow will be ready to depart.

Final Departure Time and Date Notice (Box 28 (d))
The Hirer shall give the Tugowner the number of days notice of the time and date of sailing of the Tow which day shall fall within the final departure period.

Notices to be given to (Box 28 (e))
The above notices shall be give by the Hirer to the addressee mentioned in Box 28 (e).

PART II
"Towcon" International Ocean Towage Agreement (Lump Sum)

1. **The Tow**
"The Tow" shall include any vessel, craft or object of whatsoever nature including anything carried thereon as described in PART I to which the Tugowner agrees to render the service(s) as set out in Box 22.

2. **Price and Conditions of Payment**
(a) The Hirer shall pay the Tugowner the sum set in Box 32 (hereinafter called "the Lump Sum").
(b) The Lump Sum shall be payable as set out in Boxes 32 and 33.
(c) The Lump Sum and all other sums payable to the Tugowner under this Agreement shall be payable without any discount, deduction, set-off, lien, claim or counter-claim, each instalment of the Lump Sum shall be fully and irrevocably earned at the moment it is due as set out in Box 32, Tug and/or Tow lost or not lost, and all other sums shall be fully and irrevocably earned on a daily basis.
(d) All payments by the Hirer shall be made in the currency and to the bank account specified in Box 33.
(e) In the event that the average price per metric tonne of bunkers actually paid by the Tugowner differs from the amounts specified in Box 36 then the Hirer or the Tugowner, as the case may be, shall pay to the other the difference per metric tonne for every metric tonne consumed during the voyage. The average price specified above shall be the average of the prices per metric tonne actually paid by the Tugowner on the basis of quantities purchased at the last bunkering port prior to the voyage, any bunkering port during the voyage, and the first bunkering port after completion of the voyage. The log book of the Tug shall be prima facie evidence of the quantity of bunkers consumed.
(f) Any Delay Payment due under this Agreement shall be paid to the Tugowner as and when earned on presentation of the invoice.
(g) The Free Time specified in Boxes 26 and 27 shall be allowed for the connecting and disconnecting of the Tow and all other purposes relating thereto. Free Time shall commence when the Tug arrives at the pilot station at the place of departure or the Tug and Tow arrives at the pilot station at the place of destination or anchors or arrives at the usual waiting area off such places. Should the Free Time be exceeded, Delay Payment(s) at the rate specified in Box 29 shall be payable until the Tug and Tow sail from the place of departure or the Tug is free to leave the place of destination.

3. **Additional Charges and Extra Costs**
(a) The Hirer shall appoint his agents at the place of departure and place of destination and ports of call or refuge and shall provide such agents with adequate funds as required.
(b) The Hirer shall bear and pay as and when they fall due:-
(i) All port expenses, pilotage charges, harbour and canal dues and all other expenses of a similar nature levied upon or payable in respect of both the Tug and the Tow.
(ii) All taxes, (other than those normally payable by the Tugowner in the country where he has his principal place of business and in the country where the Tug is registered) stamp duties or other levies payable in respect of or in connection with this Agreement or the payments of the Lump Sum or other sums payable under this Agreement or the services to be performed under or in pursuance of this Agreement, any Customs or Excise duties and taxes, dues or expenses payable in respect of any necessary permits or licences.
(iii) The cost of the services of any assisting tugs when deemed necessary by the Tugmaster or prescribed by Port or other Authorities.
(iv) All costs and expenses necessary for the preparation of the Tow for towing (including such costs or expenses as those of raising the anchor of the Tow or tending or casting off any moorings of the Tow).
(v) The cost of insurance of the Tow shall be the sole responsibility of the Hirer to provide.
(c) All taxes, charges, costs, and expenses payable by the Hirer shall be paid by the Hirer direct to those entitled to such payment. If, however, any such tax, charge, cost or expense is in fact paid by or on behalf of the Tugowner (notwithstanding that the Tugowner shall under no circumstances be under any obligation to make such payments on behalf of the Hirer) the Hirer shall reimburse the Tugowner on the basis of the actual cost to the Tugowner upon presentation of invoice.

4. **War Risk Escalation Clause**
The Lump Sum is based and assessed on all war risk insurance costs applicable to the Tugowner in respect of the contemplated voyage in effect on the date of this Agreement.
In the event of any subsequent increase or decrease in the actual costs due to the Tugowner fulfilling his obligations under this Agreement, the Hirer or the Tugowner, as the case may be, shall reimburse to the other the amount of any increase or decrease in the war risk, confiscation, deprivation or trapping insurance costs.

5. **Interest**
If any amounts due under this Agreement are not paid when due, then interest shall accrue and shall be paid in accordance with the provisions of Box 34, on all such amounts until payment is received by the Tugowner.

6. **Security**
The Hirer undertakes to provide, if required by the Tugowner, security to the satisfaction of the Tugowner in the form and in the sum, at the place and at the time indicated in Box 35 as a guarantee for due performance of the Agreement. Such security shall be returned to the guarantor when the Hirer's financial obligations under this Agreement have been met in full.
(Optional, only applicable if Box 35 filled in).

7. **Place of Departure/Notices**
(a) The Tow shall be tendered to the Tugowner at the place of departure stated in Box 24.
(b) The precise place of departure shall always be safe and accessible for the Tug to enter, to operate in and for the Tug and Tow to leave and shall be a place where such Tug is permitted to commence the towage in accordance with any local or other rules, requirements or regulations and shall always be subject to the approval of the Tugowner which shall not be unreasonably withheld.
(c) (i) The Tow shall be ready to sail from the Place of Departure between the dates indicated in Box 28 (a), hereinafter called the Initial Departure Period.
(ii) The Hirer shall give the Tugowner such notice as is stipulated in Box 28 in respect of Initial Departure Notice (Box 28 (b)), Final Departure Period Notice (Box 28 (c)) and Final Departure Time and Date Notice (Box 28 (d)).
(iii) The Tow shall be offered to the Tugowner, duly certificated and otherwise in accordance with the terms and conditions of this Agreement.
(d) If the Hirer fails to comply strictly with the provisions of Cl. 7(c) the date of departure shall be deemed to be either the last day of the Initial Departure Period or the last day of the Final Departure Period, whichever is earlier, and this date shall be binding for all consequences arising in respect of Delay Payments and any other payments due or charges incurred in the performance of this Agreement.

8. **Place of Destination**
(a) The Tow shall be accepted forthwith and taken over by the Hirer or his duly authorised representative at the place of destination stated in Box 25.
(b) The precise place of destination shall always be safe and accessible for the Tug and Tow to enter, to operate in, and for the Tug to leave and shall be a place where such Tug is permitted to redeliver the Tow in accordance with any local or other rules, requirements or regulations and shall always be subject to the approval of the Tugowner, which approval shall not be unreasonably withheld.

9. **Riding Crew**
(a) In the event that the Tug owner provides a Riding Crew for the Tow, such crew and their suitability for the work shall be in the discretion of the Tugowner. All expenses for such personnel shall be for the account of the Tugowner.
(b) In the event that any personnel are placed on board the Tow by the Hirer all expenses for such personnel will be for the account of the Hirer and such personnel shall be at all times under the orders of the Master of the Tug, but shall not be deemed to be the servants or agents of the Tugowner.
(c) The Riding Crew shall be provided at the Hirer's sole expense with suitable accomodation, food, fresh water, life saving appliances and all other requirements to comply as necessary with the law and regulations of the law of the Flag of the Tug and/or Tow and of the States through the territorial waters of which the Tug will pass or enter. It is a requirement that members of the Riding Crew provided by the Hirer shall be able to speak and understand the English language or any other mutual language.

10. **Towing Gear and Use of Tow's Gear**
(a) The Tugowner agrees to provide free of cost to the Hirer all towing hawsers, bridles and other towing gear normally carried on board the Tug, for the purpose of the towage or other services to be provided under this Agreement. The Tow shall be connected up in a manner within the discretion of the Tugowner.
(b) The Tugowner may make reasonable use at his discretion of the Tow's gear, power, anchors, anchor cables, radio, communication and naviga-

PART II
"Towcon" International Ocean Towage Agreement (Lump Sum)

tional equipment and all other appurtenances free of cost during and for the purposes of the towage or other services to be provided under this Agreement.

11. Permits and Certification
(a) The Hirer shall arrange at his own cost and provide to the Tugowner all necessary licenses, authorisations and permits required by the Tug and Tow to undertake and complete the contractual voyage together with all necessary certification for the Tow to enter or leave all or any ports of call or refuge on the contemplated voyage.
(b) Any loss or expense incurred by the Tugowner by reason of the Hirer's failure to comply with this Clause shall be reimbursed by the Hirer to the Tugowner and during any delay caused thereby the Tugowner shall receive additional compensation from the Hirer at the Tug's Delay Payment rate specified in Box 29.

12. Tow-worthiness of the Tow
(a) The Hirer shall exercise due diligence to ensure that the Tow shall, at the commencement of the towage, be in all respects fit to be towed from the place of departure to the place of destination.
(b) The Hirer undertakes that the Tow will be suitably trimmed and prepared and ready to be towed at the time when the Tug arrives at the place of departure and fitted and equipped with such shapes, signals, navigational and other lights of a type required for the towage.
(c) The Hirer shall supply to the Tugowner or the Tugmaster, on the arrival of the Tug at the place of departure an unconditional certificate of tow-worthiness for the Tow issued by a recognised firm of Marine Surveyors or Survey Organisation, provided always that the Tugowner shall not be under any obligation to perform the towage until in his discretion he is satisfied that the Tow is in all respects trimmed, prepared, fit and ready for towage but the Tugowner shall not unreasonably withhold his approval.
(d) No inspection of the Tow by the Tugowner shall constitute approval of the Tow's condition or be deemed a waiver of the foregoing undertakings given by the Hirer.

13. Seaworthiness of the Tug
The Tugowner will exercise due diligence to tender the Tug at the place of departure in a seaworthy condition and in all respects ready to perform the towage, but the Tugowner gives no other warranties, express or implied.

14. Substitution of Tugs
The Tugowner shall at all times have the right to substitute any tug or tugs for any other tug or tugs of adequate power (including two or more tugs for one, or one tug for two or more) at any time whether before or after the commencement of the towage or other services and shall be at liberty to employ a tug or tugs belonging to other tugowners for the whole or part of the towage or other service contemplated under this Agreement. Provided however, that the main particulars of the substituted tug or tugs shall be subject to the Hirer's prior approval, but such approval shall not be unreasonably withheld.

15. Salvage
(a) Should the Tow break away from the Tug during the course of the towage service, the Tug shall render all reasonable services to re-connect the towline and fulfill this Agreement without making any claim for salvage.
(b) If at any time the Tugowner or the Tugmaster considers it necessary or advisable to seek and accept salvage services from any vessel or person on behalf of the Tug or Tow, or both, the Hirer hereby undertakes and warrants that the Tugowner or his duly authorised servant or agent including the Tugmaster have the full actual authority of the Hirer to accept such services on behalf of the Tow on any reasonable terms.

16. Cancellation and Withdrawal
(a) At any time prior to the departure of the Tow from the place of departure the Hirer may cancel this Agreement upon payment of the cancellation fee set out in Box 38. If cancellation takes place whilst the Tug is en route to the place of departure or after the Tug has arrived at or off the place of departure then in addition to the said cancellation fee the Hirer shall pay any additional amounts due under this Agreement.
(b) In the event that the towage operation is terminated after departure from the place of departure, but before the Tow arrives at the place of destination without fault on the part of the Tugowner, his servants or agents, the Tugowner shall be entitled to be paid, and if already paid to retain all sums payable according to Box 32, accrued Delay Payments and any other amounts due under this Agreement. The above amounts are in addition to any damages the Tugowner may be entitled to claim for breach of this Agreement.
(c) The Tugowner may without prejudice to any other remedies he may have leave the Tow in a place where the Hirer may take repossession of it and be entitled to payment of the Lump Sum less expenses saved by the Tugowner and all other payments due under this Agreement, upon any one or more of the following grounds:
(i) If there is any delay or delays (other than delay caused by the Tug) at the place of departure exceeding in aggregate 21 running days.
(ii) If there is any delay or delays (other than a delay caused by the Tug) at any port or place of call or refuge exceeding in aggregate 21 running days.
(iii) If the security as may be required according to Box 35 is not given within 7 running days of the Tugowner's request to provide security.
(iv) If the Hirer has not accepted the Tow within 7 running days of arrival at the place of destination.
(v) If any amount payable under this Agreement has not been paid within 7 running days of the date such sums are due.
(d) Before exercising his option of withdrawing from this Agreement as aforesaid, the Tugowner shall if practicable give the Hirer 48 hours notice (Saturdays, Sundays and public Holidays excluded) of his intention to so withdraw.
(e) Should the Tug not be ready to commence the towage at the latest at midnight on the date, if any, indicated in Box 37, the Hirer shall have the option of cancelling this Agreement and shall be entitled to claim damages for detention if due to the wilful default of the Tugowner. Should the Tugowner anticipate that the Tug will not be ready, he shall notify the Hirer thereof by telex, cable or otherwise in writing without delay stating the expected date of the Tug's readiness and ask whether the Hirer will exercise his option to cancel. Such option to cancel must be exercised within 48 hours after the receipt of the Tugowner's notice, otherwise the third day after the date stated in the Tugowner's notice shall be deemed to be the new agreed date to commence the towage in accordance with this Agreement.

17. Necessary Deviation or Slow Steaming
(a) If the Tug during the course of the towage or other service under this Agreement puts into a port or place or seeks shelter or is detained or deviates from the original route as set out in Box 23, or slow steams because either the Tugowner or Tugmaster reasonably consider
(i) that the Tow is not fit to be towed or
(ii) the Tow is incapable of being towed at the original speed contemplated by the Tugowner or
(iii) the towing connection requires rearrangement, or
(iv) repairs or alterations to or additional equipment for the Tow are required to safeguard the venture and enable the Tow to be towed to destination, or
(v) it would not be prudent to do otherwise on account of weather conditions actual or forecast, or
because of any other good and valid reason outside the control of the Tugowner or Tugmaster, or because of any delay caused by or at the request of the Hirer, this Agreement shall remain in full force and effect, and the Tugowner shall be entitled to receive from the Hirer additional compensation at the appropriate Delay Payment rate as set out in Box 29 for all time spent in such port or place and for all time spent by the Tug at sea in excess of the time which would have been spent had such slow steaming or deviation not taken place.
(b) The Tug shall at all times be at liberty to go to the assistance of any vessel in distress for the purpose of saving life or property or to call at any port or place for bunkers, repairs, supplies, or any other necessaries or to land disabled seamen, but if towing the Tug shall leave the Tow in a safe place and during such period this Agreement shall remain in full force and effect.
(c) The Tug shall have liberty to comply with any orders or directions as to departure, arrival, routes, ports of call, stoppages, destination, delivery, requisition or otherwise howsoever given by the Government of the Nation under whose flag the Tug or Tow sails or any department thereof, or any person acting or purporting to act with the authority for such Government or any department thereof by the committee or person having under the terms of the War Risks Insurance on the Tug the right to give such orders or directions and if by reason of and in compliance with any such orders or directions anything is done or is not done the same shall not be deemed a deviation and delivery in accordance with such orders or directions shall be a fulfilment of this Agreement and the Lump Sum and/or all other sums shall be paid to the Tugowner accordingly.
(d) Any deviation howsoever or whatsoever by the Tug or by the Tugowner not expressly permitted by the terms and conditions of this Agreement shall not amount to a repudiation of this Agreement and the Agreement shall remain in full force and effect notwithstanding such deviation.

18. Liabilities

1. Date and place of Agreement	RECOMMENDED INTERNATIONAL OCEAN TOWAGE AGREEMENT (D A I L Y H I R E) CODE NAME: "TOWHIRE" PART I
2. Tugowner/place of business	3. Hirer/place of business
4. Tow (name and type)	5. Gross tonnage/displacement tonnage
6. Maximum length/maximum breadth & towing draught (fore and aft)	7. Flag and place of registry
8. Registered owners	9. Classification society
10. P. & I. liability insurers	11. General condition of tow
12. Particulars of cargo and/or ballast and/or other property on board the tow	
13. Tug (name and type)	14. Flag and place of registry
15. Gross tonnage	16. Classification society
17. P. & I. liability insurers	
18. Certificated bollard pull (if any)	19. Indicated horse power
20. Estimated daily average bunker oil consumption in good weather and smooth water	
(a) at full towing power with tow	
(b) at full sea speed without tow	
21. Winches and main towing gear	

(continued)

(continued)   "TOWHIRE" INTERNATIONAL OCEAN TOWAGE AGREEMENT (DAILY HIRE)   PART I

22. Nature of service(s) (Cl. 1)	
23. Place of departure (Cl. 7) 24. Date of departure	25. Place of destination (Cl. 8)
26. Contemplated route (Cl. 17)	
27. Notices (state number of hours/days notice of arrival of tug at place of departure and to whom to be given)	28. Notices (state number of hours/days notice of arrival of tug and tow at place of destination and to whom to be given)
29. Riding crew to be provided by (also state number to be provided) (Cl. 9)	30. If riding crew provided by Tugowner state amount per man per day payable by Hirer (Cl. 9)
31. Mobilisation payment (optional, only to be filled in if expressly agreed) (Cl. 2(e))	32. Demobilisation payment (optional, only to be filled in if expressly agreed) (Cl. 2(f))
33. Daily rate of hire and advance payment period(s) (Cl. 2(a))	34. Payment of hire and for riding crew (if any) (state currency, mode of payment, place of payment and bank account) (Cl. 2(b))
35. Minimum period of hire, if any agreed	36. Commencement of period of hire (Cl. 2(a))
37. Termination of period of hire (Cl. 2(a))	38. Cancelling date, if any agreed (Cl. 16(e))
39. Interest rate (%) per annum to run from (state number of days) after any sum is due (Cl. 5)	40. Security (state sum, by whom to be provided and when) (optional, only to be filled in if expressly agreed) (Cl. 6)
41. Cost of bunker oil and lubricating oils (state whether included or excluded from daily rate of hire; if included state type of bunkers and cost per metric tonne (per litre for lubricating oils) (Cl. 2(d))	
42. Cancellation fee (Cl. 16)	43. Numbers of additional clauses, covering special provisions, if agreed

It is mutually agreed between the party mentioned in Box 2 (hereinafter called "the Tugowner") and the party mentioned in Box 3 (hereinafter called "the Hirer") that the Tugowner shall, subject to the terms and conditions of this Agreement which consists of PART I including additional clauses, if any agreed and stated in Box 43, and PART II, use his best endeavours to perform the towage or other service(s) as set out herein. In the event of a conflict of terms and conditions, the provisions of PART I and any additional clauses, if agreed, shall prevail over those of PART II to the extent of such conflict but no further.

Signature (Tugowner)	Signature (Hirer)

PART II
"Towhire" International Ocean Towage Agreement (Daily Hire)

1. The Tow
"The Tow" shall include any vessel, craft or object of whatsoever nature including anything carried thereon as described in PART 1 to which the Tugowner agrees to render the service(s) as set out in Box 22.

2. Price and Conditions of Payment
(a) The Hirer shall pay the Tug owner the amount of hire set out in Box 33 per day or pro rata for part of a day (hereinafter called the "Tug's Daily Rate of Hire") from the time stated in Box 36 until the time stated in Box 37.
(b)(i) The Tug's Daily Rate of Hire shall be payable in advance as set out in Box 33; all hire or equivalent compensation hereunder shall be fully and irrevocably earned and non-returnable on a daily basis.
(ii) In the event of the Tug being lost, hire shall cease as of the date of the loss. If the date of the loss cannot be ascertained, then, in addition to any other sums which may be due, half the rate of hire shall be paid, calculated from the date the Tug was last reported until the calculated arrival of the Tug at her destination provided such period does not exceed 14 days.
(iii) In the event of the Tow being lost, hire shall continue until the Tug arrives at its destination or such nearer place, at the Tugowner's discretion, provided such period does not exceed 14 days.
(c) Within 14 days of the termination of the services hereunder by the Tugowner, the Tugowner will if necessary adjust in conformance with the terms of this Agreement hire paid in advance. Any hire paid by the Hirer but not earned under this Agreement and which is refundable thereunder shall be refunded to the Hirer within 14 days thereafter.
(d) (i) In the event that the Daily Rate of Hire includes the cost of bunkers and the average price per metric tonne of bunkers actually paid by the Tugowner differs from the amounts specified in Box 41 then the Hirer or the Tugowner, as the case may be, shall pay to the other the difference per metric tonne for every metric tonne consumed during the voyage.
The average price specified above shall be the average of the prices per metric tonne actually paid by the Tugowner on the basis of quantities purchased at the last bunkering port prior to departure on the voyage, any bunkering port during the voyage, and the first bunkering port after completion of the voyage. The log book of the Tug shall be prima facie evidence of the quantity of bunkers consumed.
(ii) In the event that the Daily Rate of Hire excludes the cost of bunkers then the Hirer shall pay to the Tugowner the cost of the bunkers and lubricants consumed by the Tug in fulfilling the terms of this Agreement.
The Tug shall be delivered with sufficient bunkers and lubricants on board for the tow to the first bunkering port (if any) or destination and be re-delivered with not less than sufficient bunkers to reach the next bunkering stage en route to the Tug's next port of call. The Hirer upon delivery and the Tugowner upon re-delivery shall pay for the bunkers and lubricants on board at the current contract price at the time at the port of delivery and re-delivery or at the nearest bunkering port.
*) (e) If agreed, the Hirer shall pay the sum set out in Box 3l by way of a mobilisation charge. This sum shall be paid on or before the commencement of the Tug's voyage to the place of departure, and shall be non-returnable, Tug and/or Tow lost or not lost.
*) (f) if agreed, the Hirer shall pay the sum set out in Box 32 by way of a demobilisation charge. This amount shall be paid tow lost or not lost, on or before the termination by the Tugowner of his services under this Agreement.
(g) The Hire and any other sums payable to the Tug owner under this Agreement (or any part thereof) shall be due, payable and paid without any discount, deduction, set-off, lien, claim or counterclaim.
*) Sub-clauses (e) and (f) are optional and shall only apply if agreed and stated in Boxes 31 and 32, respectively.

3. Additional Charges and Extra Costs
(a) The Hirer shall appoint his agents at the place of departure and place of destination and ports of call or refuge and shall provide such agents with adequate funds as required.
(b) The Hirer shall bear and pay as and when they fall due:-
(i) All port expenses, pilotage charges, harbour and canal dues and all other expenses of a similar nature levied upon or payable in respect of both the Tug and the Tow.
(ii) All taxes, (other than those normally payable by the Tugowner in the country where he has his principal place of business and in the country where the Tug is registered) stamp duties or other levies payable in respect of or in connection with this Agreement or the payments of hire or other sums payable under this Agreement or the services to be performed under or in pursuance of this Agreement, any Customs or Excise duties and any costs, dues or expenses payable in respect of any necessary permits or licences.
(iii) The cost of the services of any assisting tugs when deemed necessary by the Tugmaster or prescribed by Port or other Authorities.
(iv) All costs and expenses necessary for the preparation of the Tow for towing (including such costs or expenses as those of raising the anchor of the Tow or tending or casting off any moorings of the Tow).
(v) The cost of insurance of the Tow shall be the sole responsibility of the Hirer to provide.
(c) All taxes, charges, costs, and expenses payable by the Hirer shall be paid by the Hirer direct to those entitled to them. If, however, any such tax, charge, cost or expense is in fact paid by or on behalf of the Tugowner (notwithstanding that the Tugowner shall under no circumstances be under any obligation to make such payments on behalf of the Hirer) the Hirer shall reimburse the Tugowner on the basis of the actual cost to the Tugowner upon presentation of invoice.

4. War Risk Escalation Clause
The rate of hire is based and assessed on all war risk insurance costs applicable to the Tugowner in respect of the contemplated voyage in effect on the date of this Agreement.
In the event of any subsequent increase or decrease in the actual costs due to the Tugowner fulfilling his obligations under this Agreement, the Hirer or the Tugowner, as the case may be, shall reimburse to the other the amount of any increase or decrease in the war risk, confiscation, deprivation or trapping insurance costs.

5. Interest
If any amounts due under this Agreement are not paid when due, then interest shall accrue and shall be paid in accordance with the provisions of Box 39, on all such amounts until payment is received by the Tugowner.

6. Security
The Hirer undertakes to provide, if required by the Tugowner, security to the satisfaction of the Tugowner in the form and in the sum, at the place and at the time indicated in Box 40 as a guarantee for due performance of the Agreement. Such security shall be returned to the guarantor when the Hirer's financial obligations under this Agreement have been met in full.
(Optional, only applicable if Box 40 filled in).

7. Place of Departure
(a) The Tow shall be tendered to the Tugowner at the place of departure stated in Box 23.
(b) The precise place of departure shall always be safe and accessible for the Tug to enter, to operate in and for the Tug and Tow to leave and shall be a place where such Tug is permitted to commence the towage in accordance with any local or other rules, requirements or regulations and shall always be subject to the approval of the Tugowner which shall not be unreasonably withheld.

8. Place of Destination
(a) The Tow shall be accepted forthwith and taken over by the Hirer or his duly authorised representative at the place of destination stated in Box 25.
(b) The precise place of destination shall always be safe and accessible for the Tug and Tow to enter, to operate in, and for the Tug to leave and shall be a place where such Tug is permitted to redeliver the Tow in accordance with any local or other rules, requirements or regulations and shall always be subject to the approval of the Tugowner, which approval shall not be unreasonably withheld.

9. Riding Crew
(a) In the event that the Tugowner provides a Riding Crew for the Tow, such crew and their suitability for the work shall be in the discretion of the Tugowner. All expenses for such personnel shall be for the account of the Tugowner.
(b) In the event that any personnel are placed on board the Tow by the Hirer all expenses for such personnel will be for the account of the Hirer and such personnel shall be at all times under the orders of the Master of the Tug, but shall not be deemed to be the servants or agents of the Tugowner.
(c) The Riding Crew shall be provided at the Hirer's sole expense with suitable accommodation, food, fresh water, life saving appliances and all other requirements to comply as necessary with the law and regulations of the law of the Flag of the Tug and/or Tow and of the States through the territorial waters of which the Tug will pass or enter. It is a requirement that members of the Riding Crew provided by the Hirer shall be able to speak and understand the English language or any other mutual language.

4. Contrato de salvamento

En términos marítimos, se considera "salvamento" aquella operación en la que un buque ofrece servicios a otro para salvar la carga, tripulación y/o el propio buque en peligro, no necesariamente inminente. Es necesario cumplir alguno de los siguientes tres requisitos para que la operación se considere de salvamento:

- Que la propiedad se halle en peligro
- Que el salvamento sea beneficioso para la propiedad salvada.
- Que la operación resulte efectiva.

El concepto de salvamento marítimo, tal y como es conocido en la actualidad, tiene su origen en el siglo XIX, cuando el desarrollo y evolución del transporte marítimo provoca mayores riesgos en el ejercicio de la navegación, lo que supone un aumento de siniestros y catástrofes en el mar. Dicho concepto de salvamento marítimo incluye dos tipos de servicios: el salvamento de un buque que se mantiene a flote, pero que se encuentra en problemas y precisa de ayuda, conocido como *dry salvage* (salvamento seco), o el rescate de un buque hundido o partido, conocido como *wet salvage* (salvamento húmedo).

Además de la embarcación, los pasajeros, la tripulación y la mercancía son también elementos propios del salvamento; por una parte, la prestación de auxilio a las vidas humanas es obligatorio, y, por otra parte, en ocasiones el valor de las mercancías transportadas puede llegar a superar al valor del buque.

En principio estos servicios no implican la existencia de un contrato; no obstante, la mayoría de las operaciones de salvamento se regulan por el formulario tipo de la *Lloyd's Open Form for Salvage Agreement (LOF)*, contrato con la premisa "*No Cure, No Pay*" ("Sin salvamento, no hay remuneración"). En las páginas siguientes se muestra un modelo de este tipo de contrato.

LOF 2000

LLOYD'S STANDARD FORM OF SALVAGE AGREEMENT

(APPROVED AND PUBLISHED BY THE COUNCIL OF LLOYD'S)

NO CURE - NO PAY

1. Name of the salvage Contractors: (referred to in this agreement as "the Contractors")	2. Property to be salved: The vessel: her cargo freight bunkers stores and any other property thereon but excluding the personal effects or baggage of passengers master or crew (referred to in this agreement as "the property")
3. Agreed place of safety:	4. Agreed currency of any arbitral award and security (if other than United States dollars)
5. Date of this agreement	6. Place of agreement
7. Is the Scopic Clause incorporated into this agreement? State alternative : Yes/No	
8. Person signing for and on behalf of the Contractors Signature:	9. Captain or other person signing for and on behalf of the property Signature:

A. **Contractors' basic obligation:** The Contractors identified in Box 1 hereby agree to use their best endeavours to salve the property specified in Box 2 and to take the property to the place stated in Box 3 or to such other place as may hereafter be agreed. If no place is inserted in Box 3 and in the absence of any subsequent agreement as to the place where the property is to be taken the Contractors shall take the property to a place of safety.

B. **Environmental protection:** While performing the salvage services the Contractors shall also use their best endeavours to prevent or minimise damage to the environment.

(continued on the reverse side)

C. **Scopic Clause:** Unless the word "No" in Box 7 has been deleted this agreement shall be deemed to have been made on the basis that the Scopic Clause is not incorporated and forms no part of this agreement. If the word "No" is deleted in Box 7 this shall not of itself be construed as a notice invoking the Scopic Clause within the meaning of sub-clause 2 thereof.

D. **Effect of other remedies:** Subject to the provisions of the International Convention on Salvage 1989 as incorporated into English law ("the Convention") relating to special compensation and to the Scopic Clause if incorporated the Contractors services shall be rendered and accepted as salvage services upon the principle of "no cure - no pay" and any salvage remuneration to which the Contractors become entitled shall not be diminished by reason of the exception to the principle of "no cure - no pay" in the form of special compensation or remuneration payable to the Contractors under a Scopic Clause.

E. **Prior services:** Any salvage services rendered by the Contractors to the property before and up to the date of this agreement shall be deemed to be covered by this agreement.

F. **Duties of property owners:** Each of the owners of the property shall cooperate fully with the Contractors. In particular:

   (i) the Contractors may make reasonable use of the vessel's machinery gear and equipment free of expense provided that the Contractors shall not unnecessarily damage abandon or sacrifice any property on board;

   (ii) the Contractors shall be entitled to all such information as they may reasonably require relating to the vessel or the remainder of the property provided such information is relevant to the performance of the services and is capable of being provided without undue difficulty or delay;

   (iii) the owners of the property shall co-operate fully with the Contractors in obtaining entry to the place of safety stated in Box 3 or agreed or determined in accordance with Clause A.

G. **Rights of termination:** When there is no longer any reasonable prospect of a useful result leading to a salvage reward in accordance with Convention Articles 12 and/or 13 either the owners of the vessel or the Contractors shall be entitled to terminate the services hereunder by giving reasonable prior written notice to the other.

H. **Deemed performance:** The Contractors' services shall be deemed to have been performed when the property is in a safe condition in the place of safety stated in Box 3 or agreed or determined in accordance with clause A. For the purpose of this provision the property shall be regarded as being in safe condition notwithstanding that the property (or part thereof) is damaged or in need of maintenance if (i) the Contractors are not obliged to remain in attendance to satisfy the requirements of any port or habour authority, governmental agency or similar authority and (ii) the continuation of skilled salvage services from the Contractors or other salvors is no longer necessary to avoid the property becoming lost or significantly further damaged or delayed.

I. **Arbitration and the LSSA Clauses:** The Contractors remuneration and/or special compensation shall be determined by arbitration in London in the manner prescribed by Lloyds Standard Salvage and Arbitration Clauses ("the LSSA Clauses") and Lloyd's Procedural Rules. The provisions of the LSSA Clauses and Lloyd's Procedural Rules are deemed to be incorporated in this agreement and form an integral part hereof. Any other difference arising out of this agreement or the operations hereunder shall be referred to arbitration in the same way.

J. **Governing law:** This agreement and any arbitration hereunder shall be governed by English law.

K. **Scope of authority:** The Master or other person signing this agreement on behalf of the property identified in Box 2 enters into this agreement as agent for the respective owners thereof and binds each (but not the one for the other or himself personally) to the due performance thereof.

L. **Inducements prohibited:** No person signing this agreement or any party on whose behalf it is signed shall at any time or in any manner whatsoever offer provide make give or promise to provide or demand or take any form of inducement for entering into this agreement.

<u>**IMPORTANT NOTICES :**</u>

1. **Salvage security.** As soon as possible the owners of the vessel should notify the owners of other property on board that this agreement has been made. If the Contractors are successful the owners of such property should note that it will become necessary to provide the Contractors with salvage security promptly in accordance with Clause 4 of the LSSA Clauses referred to in Clause I. The provision of General Average security does not relieve the salved interests of their separate obligation to provide salvage security to the Contractors.

2. **Incorporated provisons.** Copies of the Scopic Clause; the LSSA Clauses and Lloyd's Procedural Rules may be obtained from (i) the Contractors or (ii) the Salvage Arbitration Branch at Lloyd's, One Lime Street, London EC3M 7HA.

Tel.No. + 44(0)20 7327 5408
Fax No. +44(0)20 7327 6827
E-mail: lloyds-salvage@lloyds.com.
www.lloydsoflondon.com

5
Incoterms - Cláusulas de transporte

Introducción

El término *INCOTERMS* (*International Commercial Terms*) define el conjunto de reglas internacionales publicadas por la Cámara Internacional de Comercio de París con el fin de estandarizar la interpretación de los términos más utilizados en el comercio internacional y delimitar las condiciones internacionales de comercio sobre el reparto de costes y riesgos entre comprador y vendedor. Hoy en día están vigentes los Incoterms 2000 de la Cámara de Comercio Internacional (CCI), en la Publicación 560.

1. Los Incoterms

Los Incoterms se utilizan en los diferentes modos de transporte (marítimo, terrestre, aéreo, multimodal). Sin embargo, algunos de ellos son de uso exclusivo para el transporte por mar o por vías acuáticas de navegación interior, como son los siguientes: FAS, FOB, CFR, CIF, DES, DEQ.

En los distintos documentos utilizados para el comercio de mercancías, aparece reflejado el Incoterm que regula las condiciones acordadas por las partes, seguido del lugar convenido para la entrega de las mercancías. Un ejemplo sería el caso de un transporte de mercancías entre Francia y España, en el que habría que especificar el lugar o puerto concreto donde se realiza dicha entrega.

CUADRO-RESUMEN DE LOS INCOTERMS

E	EX	*Ex Works ... named place*	En fábrica ... lugar convenido
F	FCA	*Free Carrier ... named place*	Franco transportista ... lugar convenido
	FAS	*Free Alongside Ship... named port of shipment*	Franco al costado del barco ... puerto de carga convenido
	FOB	*Free on Board ... named port of shipment*	Franco a bordo ... puerto de carga convenido
C	CFR	*Cost and Freight ... named port of destination*	Coste y flete ... puerto de destino convenido
	CIF	*Cost, Insurance and Freight ... named port of destination*	Coste, seguro y flete ... puerto de destino convenido
	CPT	*Carriage Paid To ... named point of destination*	Transporte pagado hasta ... lugar de destino convenido
	CIP	*Carriage and Insurance Paid To ... named point of destination*	Transporte y seguros pagados hasta ... lugar de destino convenido

D	DAF	*Delivered at Frontier ... named point*	Entregado en frontera ... lugar convenido
	DES	*Delivered Ex Ship ... named port of destination*	Entregado a bordo ... puerto de destino convenido
	DEQ	*Delivered Ex Quay ... named port of destination*	Entregado en muelle ... puerto de destino convenido
	DDU	*Delivered Duty Unpaid ... named point*	Entregado sin pago de derechos ... lugar convenido
	DDP	*Delivered Duty Paid ... named point*	Entregado libre de derechos ... lugar convenido

Como puede observarse en el cuadro los términos se agrupan en cuatro categorías:

1. Término E: el único en el que el vendedor pone las mercancías a disposición del comprador en los propios locales del vendedor.

2. Términos F: al vendedor se le encarga que la entrega de mercancía se realice en el medio de transporte escogido por el comprador.

3. Términos C: el vendedor contrata el transporte, pero sin riesgos de pérdida o daño de la mercancía o de costes adicionales ocasionados tras la carga y despacho.

4. Términos D: el vendedor soporta todos los gastos y riesgos para llevar la mercancía al lugar/país de destino.

Esta clasificación muestra que la responsabilidad del vendedor sobre los costes y riesgos del transporte aumenta proporcionalmente, tal y como se refleja en el siguiente gráfico, donde aparecen señalados los Incoterms más utilizados. En el caso de que en el contrato figure acordado el Incoterm EXW, el vendedor sólo se responsabiliza de los costes y riesgos de la mercancía durante el transporte desde su fábrica, donde la pone a disposición del comprador o sus agentes, siendo éstos los responsables de asumir el transporte de dicha mercancía, asumiendo los costes y riesgos; si el Incoterm pactado es FAS, el vendedor entregará la mercancía ya despachada en Aduanas, y así sucesivamente, aumentando cada vez más el riesgo para el comprador, hasta llegar al DDP, en la que el vendedor pone a disposición la mercancía en el punto de destino, ocupándose incluso de la descarga.

CUADRO RESUMEN DE LOS INCOTERMS

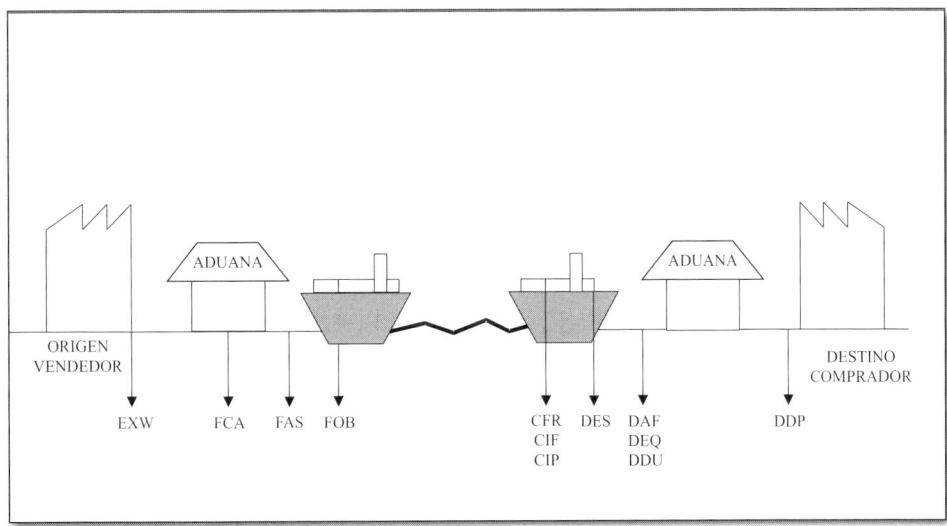

A continuación se muestran diferentes gráficos para cada uno de los Incoterms:

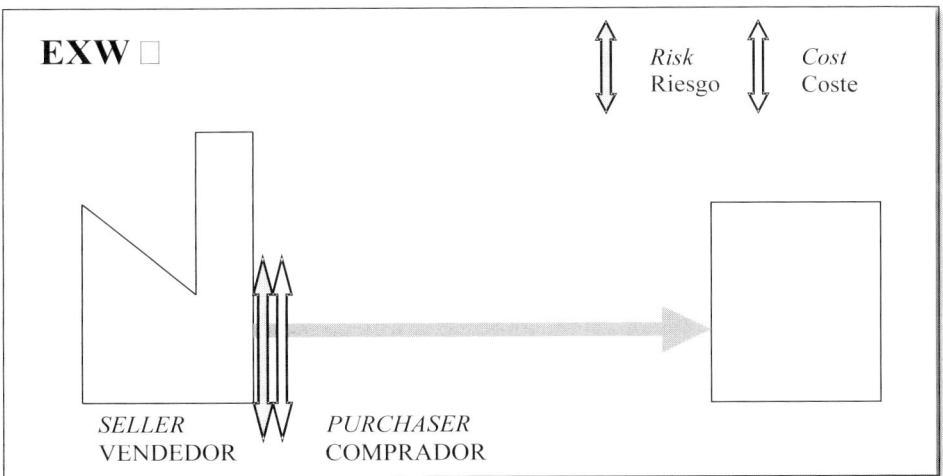

EXW: Constituye la mínima obligación para el vendedor, que realiza la entrega en su propio almacén, mientras que el comprador corre con todos los riesgos y costes inherentes al transporte de la mercancía.

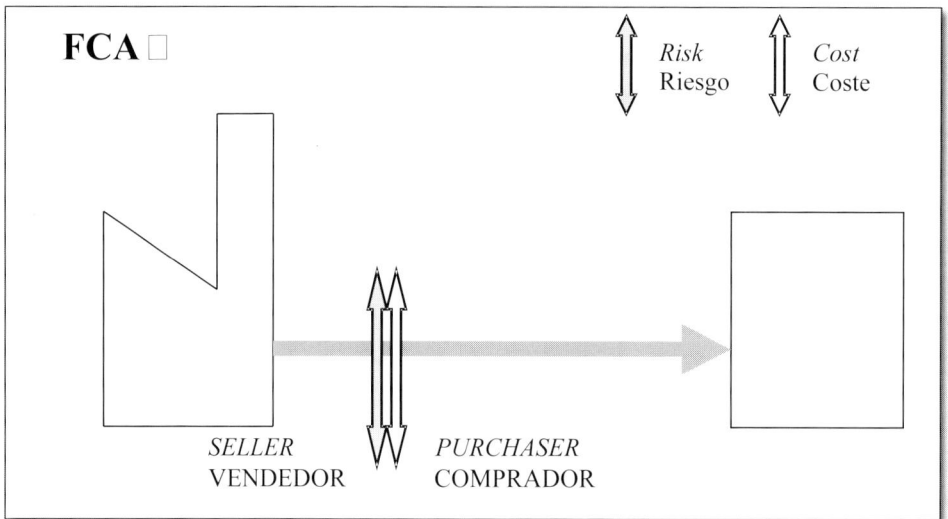

FCA: El vendedor entrega la mercancía, ya despachada en Aduanas, en el lugar convenido, momento en el que el comprador se hace cargo de la misma, corriendo con los costes y riesgos.

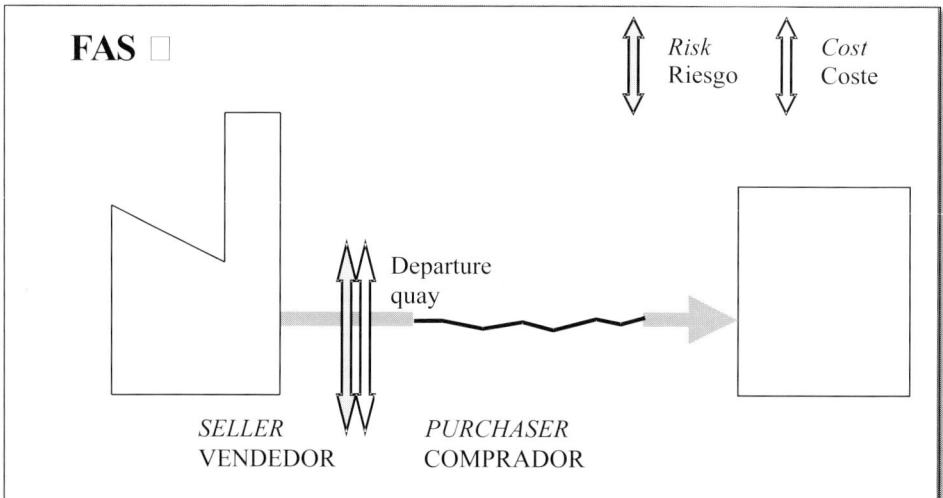

FAS: El comprador asume los costes y riesgos una vez recibida la mercancía en el puerto convenido, al costado del buque. El despacho de aduanas corre por cuenta del vendedor.

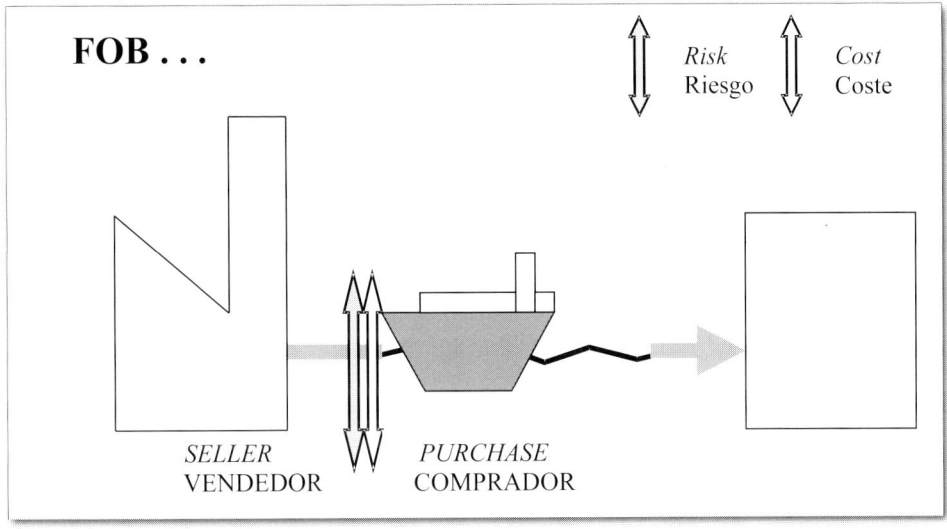

FOB: La responsabilidad del vendedor se extiende hasta el momento en que la carga es depositada a bordo del buque en el puerto convenido.

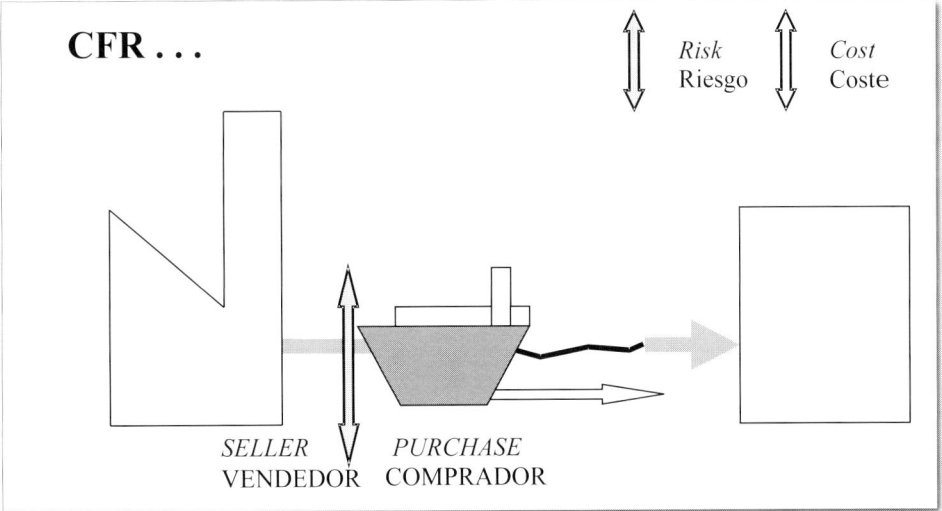

CFR: Al igual que en el caso anterior, la carga es responsabilidad del vendedor hasta su entrega a bordo del buque, quien además asume los gastos del flete marítimo.

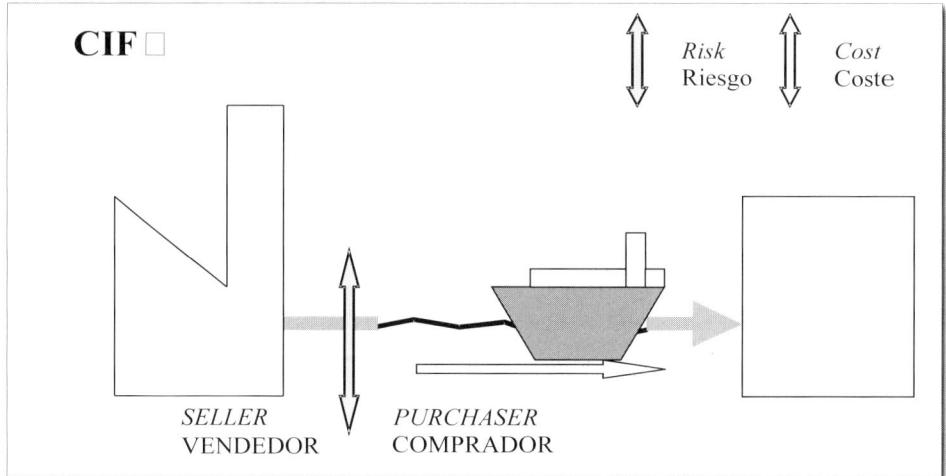

CIF: El vendedor tiene las mismas obligaciones que en el CFR, pero en este caso asume la contratación y el pago de un seguro de cobertura por pérdida o daño de la mercancía durante el transporte.

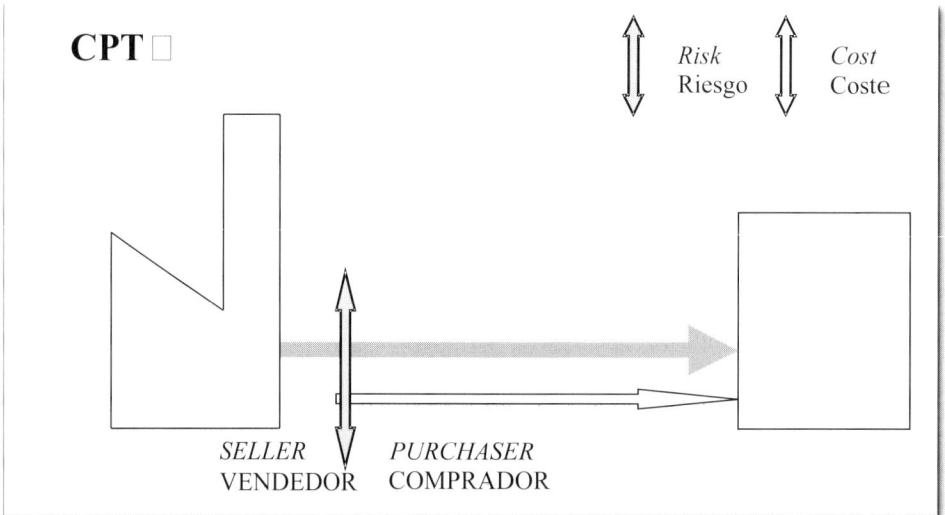

CPT: Recoge las mismas condiciones para el comprador y el vendedor que el término CFR, pero no se aplica exclusivamente para el transporte marítimo.

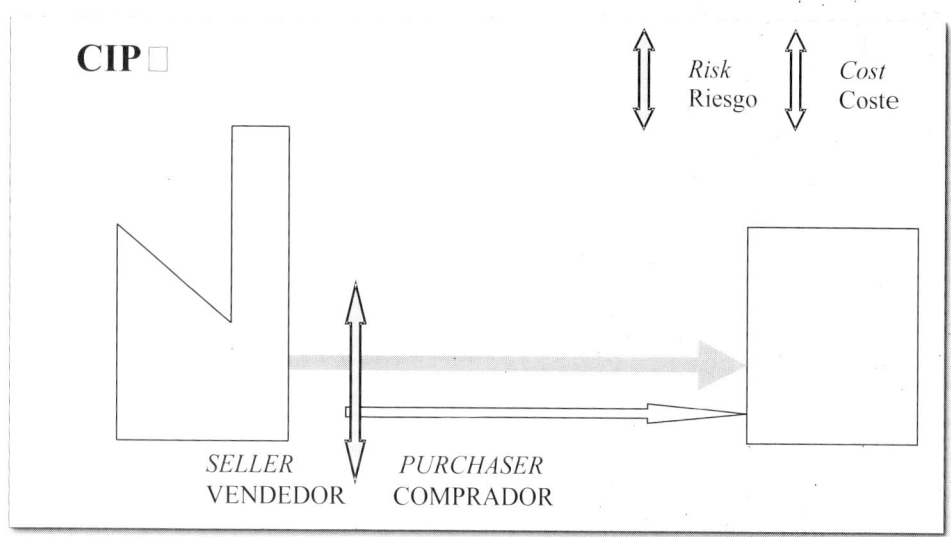

CIP: Al igual que el término CPT, obliga al vendedor al pago del flete del transporte, con la obligación añadida de incluir un seguro para las mercancías.

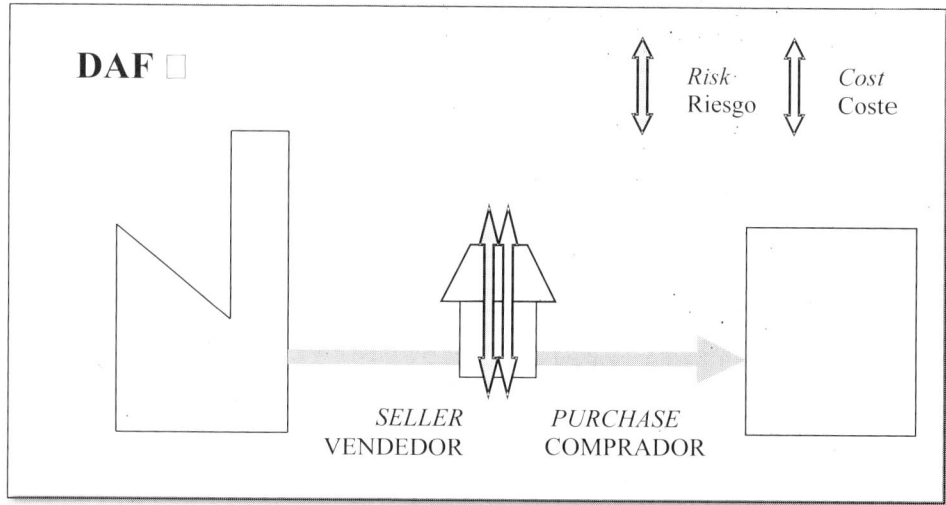

DAF: La responsabilidad del vendedor termina en el momento en que sitúa la mercancía en el punto convenido de la frontera, sin rebasar la aduana fronteriza, y sin la obligación de descargar dicha mercancía.

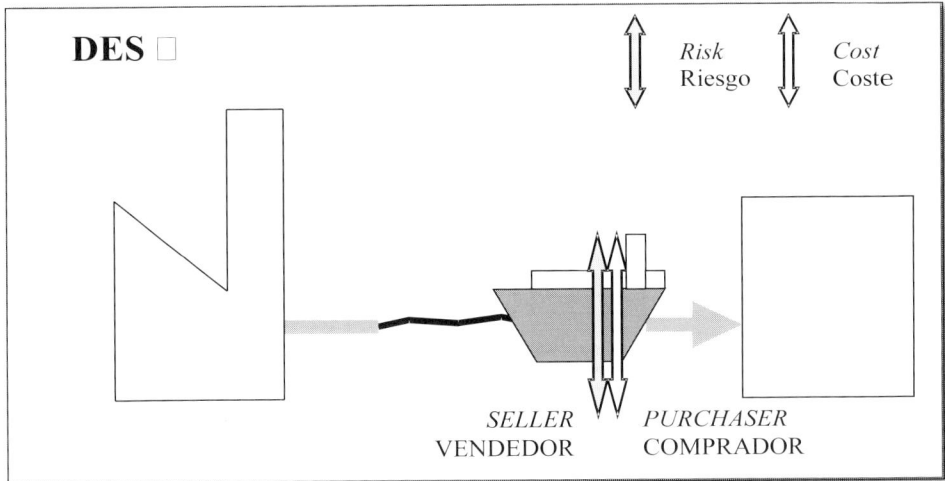

DES: El vendedor transporta la mercancía hasta el punto de destino convenido, pero no realiza la descarga ni los trámites de importación aduaneros, que corren a cargo del comprador.

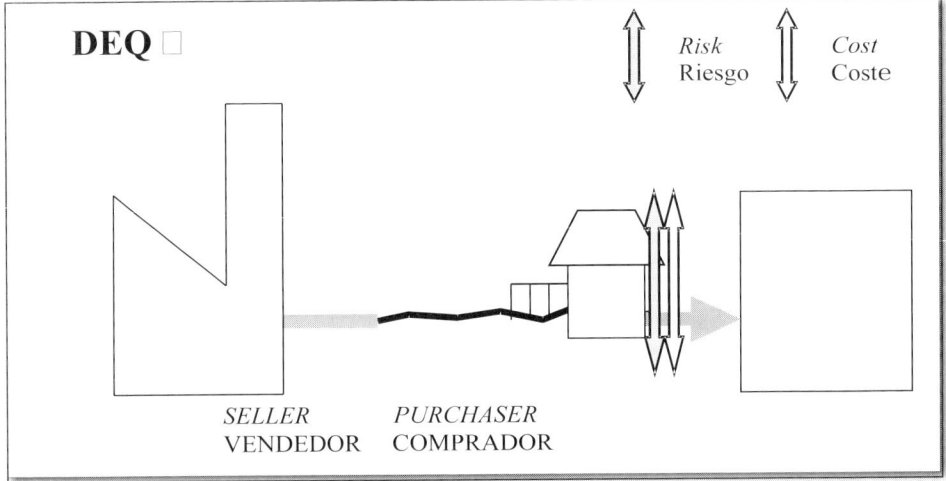

DEQ: El vendedor pone la mercancía a disposición del comprador sobre el muelle de destino y es el comprador el que corre con los gastos aduaneros de importación.

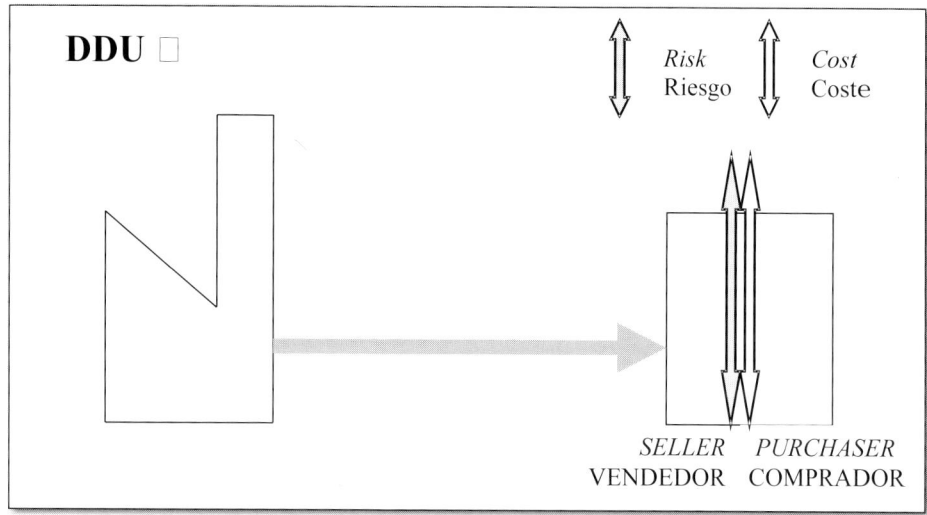

DDU: El vendedor transporta la mercancía hasta el punto convenido sin descargarla ni despacharla en la aduana.

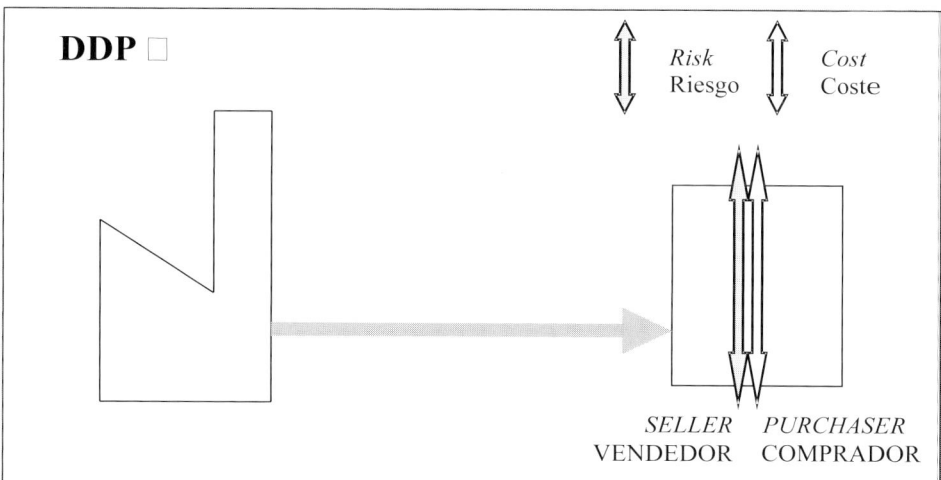

DDP: El vendedor realiza la entrega de las mercancías ya despachadas en el punto convenido, sin ocuparse de la descarga, que corre a cargo del comprador. Este término es la modalidad opuesta al EXW, pues refleja la obligación máxima del vendedor.

6
Las comunicaciones

Introducción

Las comunicaciones buque-buque, buque-tierra han de ser precisas y evitar las confusiones; por ello, en 1973 el Comité de Seguridad Marítima acordó que el inglés será la lengua utilizada en las comunicaciones marítimas.

Existen una serie de códigos y frases convencionales empleadas a la hora de establecer comunicación desde un buque, con el fin de unificar los mensajes y, en general, lograr una mayor seguridad en la actividad marítima. Estos códigos y frases, recogidos por *IMO (International Maritime Organisation)*, son conocidos como *SMCP (Standard Marine Communication Phrases-Frases Standard de Comunicación Marítima)*.

Una estandarización a tener en cuenta es en el momento en que es necesario deletrear algún término; en estos caso debería utilizarse la siguiente tabla:

LETRA	CÓDIGO	LETRA	CÓDIGO
A	Alfa	N	November
B	Bravo	O	Oscar
C	Charlie	P	Papa
D	Delta	Q	Quebec
E	Echo	R	Romeo
F	Foxtrot	S	Sierra
G	Golf	T	Tango
H	Hotel	U	Uniform
I	India	V	Victor
J	Juliet	W	Whisky
K	Kilo	X	X-ray
L	Lima	Y	Yankee
M	Mike	Z	Zulu

En lo que respecta a los dígitos, se emplea la siguiente pronunciación, con diferencias notables respecto a la pronunciación convencional.

DÍGITO	ORTOGRAFÍA	PRONUNCIACIÓN
0	Zero	Zeero
1	One	Wun
2	Two	Too
3	Three	Tree
4	Four	Fower
5	Five	Fife
6	Six	Six
7	Seven	Seven
8	Eight	Ait
9	Nine	Niner
1000	Thousand	Tousand

A la hora de comunicar tanto números como cifras sería conveniente hacer varias puntualizaciones al respecto, según la medida que indiquen:

- Siempre han de comunicarse los dígitos de uno en uno:

    Ejemplo: *"Three-Nine-Zero"* para 390

    "Five-Point-Two" para 5,2

- Si lo que se indica es latitud y longitud, se expresará en grados y minutos (y decimales de minuto si es necesario), tomando como referencia el Norte y Sur con respecto al Ecuador, y el Este y Oeste respecto a Greenwich.

    Ejemplo: *"Position 15 (One-Five) degrees 34 (Three-Four) minutes North 061 (Zero-Six-One) degrees 29 (Two-Nine) minutes West"*

Con el fin de expresar la posición de un buque, es preciso hacer referencia a los puntos cardinales, *Cardinal Points* y sus puntos intermedios, *Half Cardinal Points:*

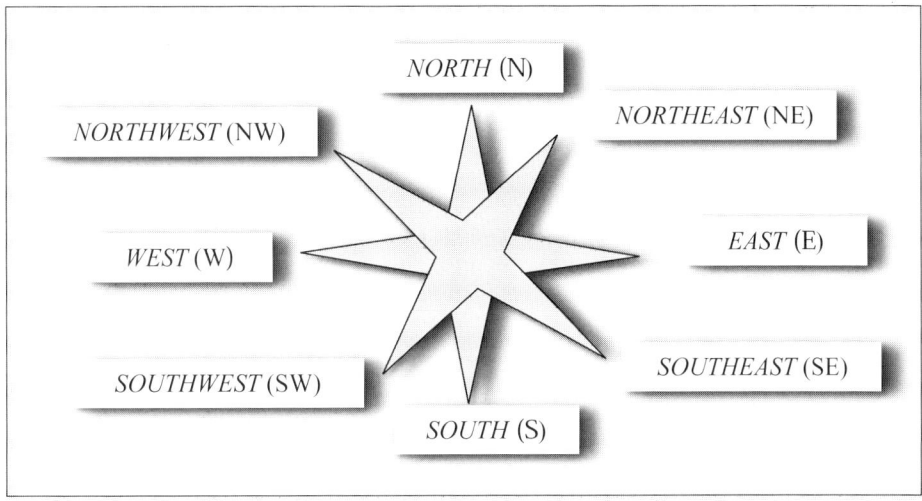

Los adjetivos correspondientes a estos términos son los siguientes:

Southern	Meridional
Northern	Septentrional
Eastern	Oriental
Western	Occidental

1. Expresiones propias de la comunicación marítima

A continuación mostramos una serie de ejemplos para las situaciones más frecuentes.

"This is ...." ...."Aquí ..."

"Over" .... "Cambio"

(Este término se repite al final de cada mensaje, para dar entrada al interlocutor).

"Out" .... "Cambio"

(Término con el que se da por finalizada la conversación).

"How do you read (me)?" (1-5) .... *"¿Cómo me oye?"*
"I read (you) bad/one" .... *"Le oigo mal"*
 poor/two .... *poco*
fair /three .... bastante bien
good/four .... bien
excellent/five" .... muy bien"

(Pueden utilizarse indistintamente los adjetivos o los numerales, ya que los numerales indican la fuerza de la señal de radio).

Es necesario proporcionar respuestas completas a las preguntas YES/NO.

"Is the fire under control?"

"Yes, fire is under control/No, fire is not under control"

"Está el fuego controlado?
"Si, el fuego está controlado/No, el fuego no está controlado"

"Stand by on VHF channel/frequency"

"Manténgase en el canal/frecuenciaVHF"

"Standing on VHF channel/frequency"

"Me mantengo en el canal/frecuenciaVHF"

"Advise switch to/change to VHF channel/frequency"

"Aconsejo cambiar al canal/frecuenciaVHF"

"Switching to/Changing to VHF channel/frequency"

"Cambio al canal/frecuenciaVHF"

2. *Message Markers*

Con el fin de mejorar la comunicación y evitar posibles confusiones, se utilizan los denominados *Message Markers* (Identificadores de mensaje), que preceden a la información y predicen el tipo de mensaje a transmitir, de los que mostramos ejemplos a continuación.

- *INSTRUCTION* (INSTRUCCIONES)

  "INSTRUCTION. Do not change your channel"

  "INSTRUCCIÓN. No cambie de canal"

- *ADVICE* (RECOMENDACIÓN)

  "ADVICE. Avoid this area"

  "CONSEJO. Evite esta área"

- *WARNING* (AVISO)

  "*WARNING. Icebergs located near your position*"

  "AVISO. Icebergs localizados cerca de su posición"

- *INFORMATION* (INFORMACION)

  "*INFORMATION. My flag State is British*"

  "INFORMACION. Mi bandera es británica"

- *QUESTION* (PREGUNTA)

  "*QUESTION. What is your position?*"

  "PREGUNTA. ¿Cuál es su posición?"

- *ANSWER* (RESPUESTA)

  "*ANSWER. My position is three-three degrees, five minutes North*"

  "RESPUESTA. Mi posición es 33 grados, cinco minutos Norte"

- *REQUEST* (PETICION)

  "*REQUEST. I require tug assistance*"

  "PETICIÓN. Preciso remolque"

- *INTENTION* (INTENCIÓN)

  "*INTENTION. I will berth port side*"

  "INTENCIÓN. Amarraré por babor"

Otras expresiones utilizadas a la hora de rectificar un mensaje son las siguientes:

"*Mistake …*" *(followed by the wrong word)*

"*Correction …*" *(followed by the right word)*

"Error…." (seguido por la palabra errónea)

"Corrección ..." (seguido por la palabra correcta)

"*My position is Southeast-Mistake*"

"*Correction. My position is Southwest*"

"Mi posición es Sureste-Error"

"Corrección. Mi posición es Suroeste"

Se pueden emplear también las siguientes expresiones:

"*Repeat*". Utilizada por el emisor para resaltar una parte concreta del mensaje.

"*Do not change position-**repeat**-Do not change position*"

"No cambie su posición-**repito**-No cambie su posición"

"*Say again*". Utilizada por el emisor para solicitar la repetición del mensaje

"*My speed is 10 knots*"

"*Say again, please*"

"*My speed is 10 knots*"

"Mi velocidad es 10 nudos"

"Repita, por favor"

"Mi velocidad es 10 nudos"

"Please spell". Solicita al interlocutor que deletree el mensaje o parte de éste
"I am near Corrubedo"
"Please spell"
"c-o-r-r-u-b-e-d-o"

"Estoy próximo a Corrubedo"
"Deletree, por favor"
"c-o-r-r-u-b-e-d-o"

"Please read back". Solicita al interlocutor que repita el mensaje recibido
"Expected arrival at 09.30"
"OK"
"Please read back"
"Expected arrival at 09.30"

"Llegada prevista a las 09.30"
"De acuerdo"
"Por favor repita"
"Llegada prevista a las 09.30"

3. Identificadores de emergencia

Existen también distintos mensajes codificados (Identificadores de emergencia), emitidos desde un buque, que indican determinadas circunstancias de peligro:

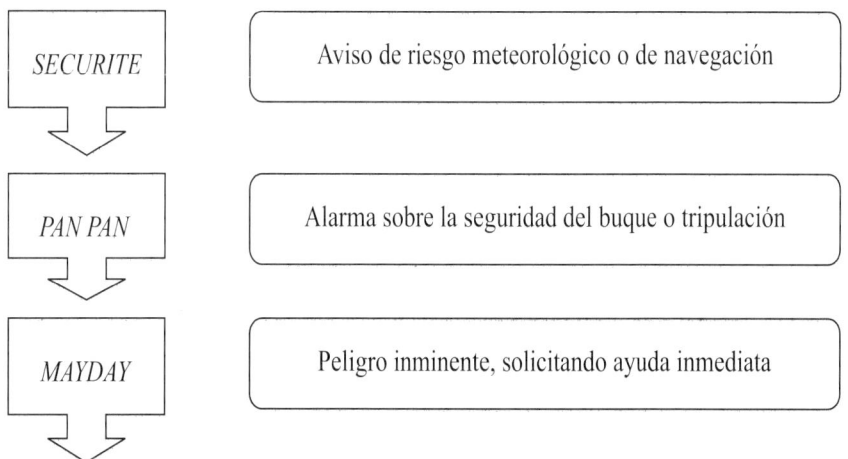

Cada una de estas expresiones se repite tres veces antes de la emisión del mensaje; junto con la expresión *ALL STATIONS* o *ALL SHIPS*.

"PAN PAN. PAN PAN. PAN PAN.
ALL STATIONS. ALL STATIONS. ALL STATIONS.
This is Motorvessel Medea.
My position is two-nine degrees, eight minutes South.
I am on fire.
I require fire-fighting assistance"

"PAN PAN. PAN PAN. PAN PAN.
A TODAS LAS ESTACIONES. A TODAS LAS ESTACIONES. A TODAS LAS ESTACIONES
Aquí Buque Medea.
Mi posición es 29 grados, ocho minutos Sur.
Fuego a bordo.
Preciso asistencia contra-incendios"

7
La meteorología

Introducción

La meteorología, como ciencia que estudia los fenómenos atmosféricos, es una fuente vital de datos para la navegación, ya que proporciona la información climatológica necesaria para la realización de las distintas actividades marítimas.

Gracias a la revolución tecnológica actual, los avances en esta materia han sido significativos, lo que hace que las predicciones meteorológicas sean cada vez más fiables y precisas, previniendo, en muchas ocasiones, situaciones de riesgo para el buque y su tripulación.

Existen escalas, estandarizadas a nivel internacional, que miden distintos fenómenos atmosféricos, como la fuerza del viento o la fuerza del mar.

1. Escala Beaufort

El almirante inglés Francis Beaufort creó en 1804 la Escala Beaufort que mide la fuerza o velocidad del viento. Años más tarde, en 1874, el Comité Meteorológico Internacional adoptó dicha escala para sus predicciones.

La velocidad del viento se descompone así en 12 grados (o 12 fuerzas), desde el grado o fuerza 0 que representa la calma, hasta el grado o fuerza 12 que representa el huracán. Para obtener con exactitud la fuerza del viento en un determinado lugar o zona, hay que medir la velocidad media durante diez minutos a una altura de 10 metros sobre la superficie del mar, en un lugar llano y despejado.

El cuadro siguiente muestra los distintos grados de la Escala Beaufort, con su equivalencia en Km/hora.

FUERZA	Km/hora	*ENGLISH*	SPANISH
0	0-2	*Calm wind*	Calma
1	2-6	*Light air*	Ventolina
2	7-11	*Light breeze*	Flojito
3	12-19	*Gentle breeze*	Flojo
4	20-29	*Moderate breeze*	Bonacible
5	30-39	*Fresh breeze*	Fresquito
6	40-50	*Strong breeze*	Fresco
7	51-61	*Near gale*	Frescachón
8	62-74	*Gale*	Temporal
9	75-87	*Storm gale*	Temporal fuerte
10	88-101	*Storm*	Temporal duro
11	102-117	*Violent storm*	Temporal muy duro
12	> 118	*Hurricane*	Huracán

2. Escala Douglas

La Escala Douglas, ideada por el vicealmirante Douglas y aprobada internacionalmente, mide el estado del mar, clasificando la altura del oleaje en diez grados, siendo 0 la mar calma y 10 el mar enorme.

En el cuadro siguiente se muestran los 10 grados de la Escala Douglas, expresando además el nivel equivalente en la Escala Beaufort, y el estado de la mar que indica cada grado.

GRADO	METROS	BEAUFORT	*ENGLISH*	SPANISH
0	0	0	*Calm sea*	Mar calma
1	< 25 cm	1,2	*Rippled sea*	Mar rizada
2	25-50 cm	3	*Smooth sea*	Marejadilla
3	0,5-1,25 cm	4	*Slight sea*	Marejada
4	1,25-2,5 m	5	*Moderate sea*	Fuerte marejada
5	2,5-4 m	6	*Rough sea*	Mar gruesa
6	4-6 m	7	*Very rough sea*	Mar muy gruesa
7	6-9	8,9	*High sea*	Mar arbolada
8	9-14 m	10,11	*Very high sea*	Mar montañosa
9	> 14	12	*Phenomenal sea*	Mar enorme

3. Mareas

Las mareas están producidas por los movimientos regulares y alternativos de ascenso y descenso del nivel del mar, que tienen su origen en la atracción del Sol y de la Luna.

Este ciclo se repite en periodos bien de 12 horas, mareas semidiurnas, bien de 24 horas, mareas diurnas.

Generalmente las mareas se producen en grandes extensiones marinas, ya que en mares cerrados o de poca extensión las mareas alcanzan poca altura; por el contrario, en los casos en los que la marea es fuerte, condiciona la actividad portuaria, hasta el punto de que los barcos sólo pueden entrar en puerto cuando la marea está alta y abandonarlo cuando la marea está baja.

Los buques pesqueros también tienen en cuenta el estado de la marea a la hora de planificar sus actividades, ya que algunas especies sólo pueden ser capturadas durante la pleamar, mientras que otras, como el lenguado, abundan durante la bajamar.

En el siguiente cuadro se muestra los distintos estados de la marea.

TIDE	**MAREA**
Low tide	Marea baja/bajamar
High tide	Marea alta/pleamar
Ebb tide	Marea descendente
Rising tide	Marea ascendente
Spring tide	Marea viva
Neap tide	Marea muerta

8
Maritime transport glossary

1. English-Spanish

A

Aboard: A bordo
Accounts: Cuentas, contabilidad
Accrue (to): Devengar
Acknowledgment of receipt : Acuse de recibo
Act of God: Fuerza mayor
Admiralty Law : Derecho marítimo
Adrift: A la deriva
Affreightment: Fletamento
Afloat: A flote
Aft: Popa
Agent: Agente, intermediario
Agreement: Acuerdo, contrato, convenio
Allocate (to): Asignar, dotar, repartir
Amendment: Enmienda, modificación
Anchor (to): Fondear
    Anchorage: Fondeadero
Apparel: Aparejo, equipo
Appliances: Herramientos, utensilios
Appurtenance: Compartimento, dependencia
Arbitration: Arbitraje, mediación
Arrival: Llegada
Ascertain (to): Constatar, indagar, verificar
Ashore: En tierra
Assess (to): Tasar, valorar
    Assessment: Tasación, valoración
Assignee: Cesionario
    Assignment: Cesión
Average: Avería
    General average: Avería gruesa
    Particular Average: Avería particular
Award: Sentencia, decisión arbitral

B

Bail: Fianza
   Bailee: Depositario de bienes
Bale: Bala, fardo
Ballast: Lastre
   Ballast voyage: Viaje en lastre, travesía sin carga útil
Bank guarantee: Aval, garantía bancaria
Banking days: Días hábiles, laborables
Bankruptcy: Bancarrota, quiebra
Bar: Barra, barrera
Bar (to): Prohibir, excluir
Barge: Barcaza
Beacon: Baliza
   Beaconage: Balizaje
Berth (to): Atracar, fondear
   Berth: Zona de fondeo
   Berth request: Solicitud de atraque
Bill of Lading: Conocimiento de embarque
Bill of Sale: Escritura de compraventa
Blockade/Blockage: Bloqueo
Board (to): Embarcar, subir a bordo
   Boarding: Abordaje
Boatage: Lanchaje, gastos de barco. Tasa aplicada a un buque por distintos servicios portuarios
Boiler: Caldera
Bollard: Bolardo, noray
   Bollard pull: Tracción sobre bolardo, tracción a punto fijo
Bond: Pagaré
   Bonded goods: Mercancías en depósito, sin haber pagado derechos de aduana
   In bond: En depósito, bajo dominio de la aduana
Bound to: Obligado, sujeto a
Brake Horse Power (bhp): Potencia al freno
Breach: Incumplimiento, infracción
Breadth: Anchura, manga
Breakbulk: Separación de embarques consolidados
Breaking Bulk: Comienzo de la descarga a granel

Breakwater: Rompeolas
Bridle: Cuerda de maniobra de proa
Broker: Agente marítimo
   Broker's order: Permiso de embarque
   Brokerage Commission: Comisión de corretaje
Building Contract: Contrato de construcción
Bulk: A granel
Bunker: Depósito
Bunkering: Suministro de combustible
Buoy (to): Balizar
   Buoy: Boya, baliza
   Buoyage: Balizamiento
Burden: Carga, peso muerto

C

Call at (to): Atracar, hacer escala
Cargo: Carga, mercancía
   Cargo handling: Manejo de la mercancía
   Cargo manifest: Manifiesto de carga
Carrier: Transportista
   Carriage: Gastos de transporte
   Carriage of Goods by Sea Act : Ley de Transporte Marítimo de Mercancías
Cash: Efectivo, líquido
Cast off (To): Soltar amarras
Casualty: Víctima
Chamber of Commerce: Cámara de Comercio
Chandler: Proveedor de buques
Charge (to): Cargar
   Discharge (to): Descargar
Charges: Gastos, cargas
   Charges at destination: Gastos en destino
   Charges at origin: Gastos en origen
   Collect charges: Gastos pagaderos en destino, paga el consignatario
   Packing charges: Gastos por empaque
   Prepaid charges: Gastos prepagados

Chart (to): Fletar

    Charter: Fletamento, flete

    Charter hire: Alquiler por fletamento

    Charter Party: Contrato, póliza de fletamento

    Charter period: Periodo de fletamento

    Charter rate: Tarifa de fletamento

    Charterer: Fletador

Claim (to): Demandar, reclamar

    Claim: Demanda, indemnización, petición, queja

    Claim damages: Demanda por daños y perjuicios

    Claimant: Demandante

Classification Society: Sociedad de Clasificación. Sociedad privada contratada por el armador del buque, cuya función es realizar inspecciones técnicas con la finalidad de otorgar una certificación de seguridad de la embarcación

Clause: Cláusula

    Arbitration clause: Cláusula de arbitraje

    Both to blame and collision clause: Cláusula de colisión por culpa concurrente

    Cancellation/contestable clause: Cláusula de rescisión

    Care, custody or control exclusion clause: Cláusula excluyente de responsabilidad del asegurador sobre los bienes bajo custodia del asegurado

    Cesser Clause: Cláusula en la que se establece la cesión de responsabilidad

    Constructive total loss clause: Cláusula de pérdida total virtual

    Continuation clause: Cláusula de prórroga de cobertura

    Deviation Clause: Cláusula de cambio ruta

    Free of Capture and Seizure Clause: Cláusula de riesgo de apresamiento excluido

    Free of strikes, riots and civil commotions clause: Libre de huelgas, motines y conmociones civiles

    General Average Clause: Cláusula de avería gruesa

    Guarantee Clause: Cláusula de garantía

    Institute Cargo clause: Cláusula para seguros de carga

    Landing clause: Claúsula de desembarque

    Lien Clause: Cláusula en la que se establece el derecho de retención sobre las mercancías

    New Jason clause: Cláusula restrictiva de responsabilidad del transportista

    Off hire clause: Cese de arrendamiento

    Option to consolidate: Cláusula de consolidación

Paramount clause: Cláusula de máxima importancia
Reasonable dispatch clause: Cláusula de prontitud razonable
Running down clause: Cláusula de colisión
Seaworthiness clause: Cláusula de navegabilidad
Sue and labour clause: Cláusula por la cual el asegurado debe realizar todo lo necesario después de un siniestro para evitar daños mayores
Superseding clause: Cláusula de sustitución
Warehouse to warehouse clause: Cláusula depósito a depósito

Clean on board: Libre a bordo
Clear days: Días hábiles
Clearance for customs: Despacho aduanero
Coast guard: Guardacostas
Commodity: Mercancía, productos
Compel (to): Forzar, obligar
Comply (to): Cumplir con, obedecer
  Compliance: Cumplimiento
Compulsory Acquisition: Adquisición obligatoria
Consignee: Consignatario (receptor)
Consignment: Expedición, envío, remesa
Consignor: Consignatario (emisor)
Construe (to): Interpretar
Consumable stores: Gastos generales; bienes fungibles
Contract: Contrato
  Contractor: Contratista
Conveyance: Transporte, traspaso
Cost: Costes
Counterclaim: Contrademanda
Craft: Embarcación
Crane: Grúa
  Craneman: Operario encargado de la grúa, gruísta
Crew: Tripulación
Currency: Divisa
  Current Market Price: Precio de mercado
Customs: Aduanas
  Clear (to) customs: Despachar en aduanas

Custom (to): Pagar los derechos de aduana
Custom broker: Agente, corredor de aduanas
Customs clearance: Derechos de despacho aduanero
Customs clearer/dealer: Despachante de aduanas
Customs duty: Derechos de aduana
Customs House: Aduanas
Customs tariff: Arancel de aduanas
Customary: Habitual
Customary routes: Rutas convencionales

D

Damage: Daño
Damages: Daños y perjuicios
Deadweight: Peso muerto
Deadweight tonnage (DWT): Tonelaje de peso muerto
Debarred: Inhabilitado
Deck: Cubierta
Deck cargo: Carga en cubierta, cubertada
Deck load: Cargamento sobre cubierta
On deck: En cubierta
Under deck: Bajo cubierta
Deed of convenant: Escritura de convenio
Deem (to): Considerar
Default: Negligencia, falta de cumplimiento
Delay: Retraso
Deletion: Anulación, supresión
Delivery: Entrega, abastecimiento, recepción
Delivery against acceptance (d/a): Entrega contra aceptación
Delivery against payment: Entrega contra pago
Delivery Order: Orden de entrega, talón de entrega
Overside delivery: Entrega al costado del buque
Demurrage: Demora, sobrestadía
Departure: Salida
Deprivation: Privación
Depth: Profundidad

Derrick: Grúa de brazo móvil
Deviation: Cambio de ruta
Disbursement: Desembolso
    Disbursement Account (D/A): Cuenta de escala
Disclose (to): Divulgar, revelar
Disembarkation: Desembarque
Dispatch: Despacho, expedición
Displacement tonnage: Tonelaje de desplazamiento
Disposal: Disposición
Dock (to): Atracar
    Dock: Muelle
    Dockage: Gastos de muelle
    Docking: Atraque
    Dockyard: Astillero
    Drydock: Dique seco
Draught: Calado
Dues: Cuotas
Dunnage: Material de sujeción de la carga
Duty: Arancel, derechos de aduanas, obligación
    Duty Free: Exento de aduanas, libre de impuestos

E

Enactment: Promulgación
Encumbrance: Gravamen
Endeavour (to): Procurar
Endorse (to): Avalar, endosar
    Endorsement: Endoso
Enforce (to): Ejecutar, hacer cumplir
Entitle (to): Dar derecho
    Entitled: Titular, con derecho a
Entry manifest: Manifiesto de carga
Expenditure: Gasto
Expenses: Gastos
Export: Exportación

F

Facilities: Instalaciones

Fee: Comisión, tasa

    Agency Fee: Comisión de agencia que cobra el consignatario sobre el flete

Feet: Pies

Fine: Multa, penalización

Flag: Bandera

    Flag of convenience: Bandera de conveniencia

Flat: Plataforma

Foot: Pie

Forced call: Arribo, atraque forzoso

Fore: Proa

Forecast: Previsión

Foregoing: Anterior, precedente

Forthwith: De inmediato

Forwarder/Forwarding agent: Transitario, agente de embarques

Franchise: Franquicia; porcentaje del valor asegurado del buque y/o su carga no cubierto por la compañía aseguradora

Free of expense: Sin carga económica

Free pratique: Libre plática; situación en la que la tripulación cumple los requisitos sanitarios para poder acceder al puerto de llegada y realizar actividades comerciales

Freight: Flete. Importe acordado por el alquiler de una nave o parte de ella para el transporte de mercancías, pasajeros, etc.

    Advanced freight: Flete pagado por adelantado

    Backfreight: Flete de regreso, flete de vuelta (Flete adicional pagadero al transportista por devolución de mercancía no aceptada en destino)

    Deadfreight: Falso flete (cantidad que se paga cuando no se usa la nave o la parte de ella que se había fletado)

    Freight collect/payable on delivery: Flete pagadero en destino, una vez realizada la entrega

    Freight prepaid: Flete pagado por anticipado, en origen

    Freight rate: Tarifa de flete, tipo de flete

    Freight tax: Impuesto, gravamen por el flete

    Full freight: Flete total

    Sub-freight: Subflete

Funnel: Chimenea

G

Gang: Cuadrilla, operarios

Gear: Engranaje, equipo

    Cargo handling gear: Equipo de manejo de carga

    Cargo handling gearless: Carencia de equipo de carga por parte del buque

General Average: Avería gruesa; daño intencionado en el buque y/o carga con el fin de preservar otros bienes materiales o vidas humanas

Goods: Mercancías

    Lawful goods: Mercancías autorizadas

    Unsound goods: Mercancías defectuosas

Grace period: Período de gracia

Gross Weight: Peso Bruto

H

Handle (to): Manejar, manipular

    Cargo handling: Manejo de la carga

Harbour: Puerto

Hatch: Compuerta, escotilla

Hawser: Cabo grueso, estacha

Hazard: Obstáculo, riesgo

Hinder (to): Detener, obstaculizar

Hindrance: Impedimento, obstáculo

Hire agreement: Contrato de alquiler

Hirer: Arrendador

Hold: Bodega

Holder: Titular

Hull: Casco

I

Import: Importación

Inch: Pulgada

Inducement: Recargo adicional al buque para acceder a un puerto no habitual en su ruta, si la carga no devenga un flete suficiente

In distress: En peligro

Inland waterway: Vía navegable interior

Instalment: Plazo
Insure (to): Asegurar
   Insurance: Seguro, garantía
   Insurance broker: Agente de seguros
   Insurance policy: Póliza de seguros
   Insurant/Insured: Asegurado
   Insurer: Asegurador
Intaken: Transportado, admitido
Invoice: Factura
Issue (to): Emitir, expedir
   Issue: Emisión, expedición
   Issuer: Emisor

J

Jettison: Echazón, acción de arrojar mercancía por la borda
Joint survey: Peritaje
Joint venture: Empresa conjunta
Journey: Viaje

K

Knot: Nudo

L

Lash (to): Trincar, sujetar
Latent defects: Defectos/vicios ocultos
Lawful: Legal, legítimo, lícito
Laytime/laydays: Tiempo de plancha, estadía de un buque en puerto
Lease contract: Contrato de arrendamiento
Leakage: Derrame, fuga, vía de agua
Lender: Prestamista
Letter: Carta
   Letter of credit (L/C): Carta de crédito
   Letter of attorney/Letter of delegation: Poder
   Letter of indemnity: Garantía bancaria
Levy (to): Gravar

Levy: Embargo
Liability: Responsabilidad civil, obligación
Lien: Embargo preventivo, derecho de retención
    Lien on cargo/goods: Derecho de retención de la carga/mercancías
    Lien on a vessel: Hipoteca naval
Lighter (to): Descargar la mercancía en barcazas
    Lighter: Barcaza
    Lighterage: Lanchaje, descarga en embarcaciones menores
Lighthouse: Faro
Load (to): Cargar
    Load: Carga
Lockout: Cierre patronal
Log: Corredera, aparato mecánico o electrónico que contiene un sensor con el que se mide la velocidad y las millas navegadas
    Log book: Cuaderno de bitácora, diario de navegación
Longshoreman: Estibador
Loose cargo: Carga suelta
Loss: Pérdida
    Actual total loss: Pérdida efectiva total
    Constructive total loss: Pérdida total virtual
Lump sum: A tanto alzado

M

Maintenance: Mantenimiento
Man (to): Manejar, tripular un buque
    Manned: Equipado, tripulado
Mariner: Marino
Mark: Referencia
Master: Capitán
    Master Mariner: Capitán de la Marina Mercante
    Master warrants: Poderes del capitán
    Master's declaration: Declaración del capitán
Mate: Oficial, piloto
    Mate's receipt: Recibo del piloto
Maturity: Vencimiento

Measurement: Medida
    Measurement cargo/goods: Mercancía cargada por volumen
Merchant: Comerciante
Merchandise: Mercancía
Middleman: Intermediario
Mile: Milla
Misdelivery: Entrega errónea
Moor (to): Amarrar, anclar
    Mooring: Amarraje, anclaje, fondeadero
Mortgage (to): Hipotecar
    Mortgage: Hipoteca
    Mortgagee: Acreedor hipotecario
Motive power: Fuerza motriz
Mutiny: Motín

N

Net weight: Peso neto
No arrival, no sale: Sin llegada, no hay venta
No cure, no pay: Sin salvamento, no hay pago
Notice: Notificación
    Notice of cancellation: Notificación, aviso de cancelación
    Notice of claim: Declaración de daños
    Notice of damage: Notificación de avería
    Notice of protest: Notificación de reclamación
    Notice of readiness: Carta de alistamiento, notificación de arribo
    Notice of shipment: Declaración de embarque
    Notice to mariners: Aviso a los navegantes
Notify (to) (party): Notificar (al destinatario)
Null and void: Nulo y sin efecto

O

On behalf of: En nombre de
On board: A bordo
Order: Orden, designación
Outfit: Equipamiento

Outturn: Rendimiento neto

    Outturn weight: Peso efectivo

Outsider: Transportista independiente que realiza rutas similares a las realizadas por integrantes de conferencias marítimas, sin pertenecer a ninguna de ellas

Owner: Propietario, armador

    Disponent Owner: Armador disponente

P

Package: Carga embalada

    Packing: Embalaje

Pallet: Paleta

Parcels: Paquetes, bultos

Particulars: Mercancía detallada

Penalty: Sanción

Perform (to): Ejecutar, llevar a cabo

    Performance: Ejecución

Perishable: Perecedero

Pilferage: Hurto, pillaje

Pilot: Práctico

    Pilotage: Practicaje

Piracy: Piratería

Policy: Póliza

    Endowment policy: Póliza de seguro total

Port: Puerto

    Bunkering port: Puerto de aprovisionamiento de combustible

    Free port: Puerto franco, puerto libre

    Port duties: Derechos portuarios

    Port of call: Puerto de escala

    Port of discharge/delivery: Puerto de descarga

    Port of distress: Puerto de refugio, de recalada forzosa

    Port of loading: Puerto de carga

    Port/Harbour Authority: Autoridad Portuaria

Pre-trip: Chequeo previo de contenedores frigoríficos para asegurar su buen estado

Premium: Prima

Pro rata: En proporción

Proceeding: Trámites, procedimientos
Procurement man: Agente de compras, aprovisionamiento
Profit: Beneficio, ganancia
Property: Propiedad
Provision: Cláusula, estipulación, medida
Purchase Agreement: Contrato de venta
Pursuant to: En virtud de
Pursue (to): Proseguir, seguir
Putting back: Recalada. Vuelta al puerto por avería o diversos problemas
Putting in: Arribada. Entrada de un barco a un puerto que no es el de destino, de forma voluntaria o forzosa

Q

Quarantine: Cuarentena
Quay: Muelle
    Quayage: Derechos de muelle

R

Rate: Tarifa
Raw material: Materia prima
Receipt: Recepción, recibo
Receiver: Destinatario, receptor
Recklessly: Temerariamente
Red label: Etiqueta roja (para mercancías peligrosas)
Redelivery: Devolución, retorno
Reefer: Frigorífico, compartimento refrigerado
Registry: Registro
Regulation: Normativa, reglamento
Reimburse (to): Reembolsar
    Reimbursement: Indemnización, reembolso
Remedy: Reparación, solución
Remittance: Remesa
Renewal: Prórroga, renovación
Repossess (to): Recobrar, recuperar
Requisition: Demanda, solicitud

Retail: Venta al por menor

Reship (to): Reembarcar, reexpedir

   Reshipment: Reembarque

Restraints of labour: Restricciones laborales

Revert (to): Revertir, volver

Riders: Cláusulas particulares adicionales

Rights: Derechos

Riot: Motín

Risk: Riesgo

Round trip: Fletamento por un período de tiempo no determinado, en el que el fletador no puede apartarse de unas zonas especificadas, sin previo consentimiento del fletante

Route: Ruta, itinerario

Rule: Norma, regla

Runner: Amante, cabo grueso con un aparejo en su extremo inferior para levantar grandes pesos

Running costs: Gastos originados por la explotación comercial de un buque

Running days: Días laborables

S

Sail (to): Navegar

Salvage: Salvamento

   Salvage agreement: Contrato de salvamento

   Salvage award: Prima por el salvamento

   Salvage charges: Costes de salvamento

   Salvage reward: Recompensa, remuneración por el salvamento

   Salvor: Salvador, persona o buque que realiza operaciones de salvamento

Save (to): Salvar

Scope: Ámbito, alcance

Scuttle (to): Echar a pique, hundir intencionadamente

Sea: Mar

Sea waybill: Documento de embarque marítimo

Seal: Sello

Seaworthy: Navegable, en buen estado para la navegación

   Seaworthiness: Navegabilidad

   Unseaworthiness: Innavegable, no apto para navegar

Seizure: Apresamiento, decomiso, embargo

Servant: Empleado

Set-off: Compensación

Settlement: Acuerdo, convenio

Ship (to): Embarcar

Ship: Buque, nave

  Ship´s Clearance: Despacho del Buque, autorización sanitaria previa a la entrada y/o salida del buque en puerto

  Shipboard: A bordo

  Shipbreaker: Desguazador

  Shipbroker: Agente, corredor marítimo, corredor de buques

  Shipbuilder: Constructor naval

  Shipbuilding: Construcción naval

  Shipload: Cargamento

  Shipment: Embarque, envío

  Shipowner: Armador, naviero, propietario de un buque

  Shipper: Exportador, fletador

  Shipping company: Compañía naviera

  Shipping document: Documento de embarque

  Shipyard: Astillero

Shore: Orilla

  Shoreline: Línea de pleamar

  Shorewards: Hacia la costa, hacia tierra

Short Sea Shipping: Tráfico marítimo de corta distancia

Signature: Firma

Sink (to): Hundir

Sling: Eslinga

Smooth water: Aguas tranquilas, mar en calma

Spare parts: Piezas de recambio, piezas de repuesto

Special Drawing Rights (SDR): Derechos especiales de giro (DEG). Según el Fondo Monetario Internacional (FMI), es un activo de reserva internacional creado en 1969 para complementar los activos de reserva existentes en los países miembros

Stamp duties: Derechos de franqueo

Steam (to): Navegar

  Steaming: Navegación

Steersman: Timonel
Stevedore (to): Estibar
    Stevedore: Estibador
    Stevedoring: Estiba y desestiba
Stoppage: Escala, parada
Store (to): Almacenar
    Storage: Almacenamiento, depósito
    Store: Almacén, pañol
Stow (to): Estibar, arrumar
    Stowage: Estiba, arrumaje
    Stowage Plan: Plano de estiba en el que se indica el orden y colocación de las mercancías dentro de un buque
Strand (to): Encallar
Strike: Huelga
Sublet: Subarriendo, subcontrato
Suit at law: Litigio ante los tribunales
Summer freeboard: Francobordo de verano
Summer load line: Línea de carga de verano
Supply (to): Proveer
    Supplier: Proveedor
Surrender (to): Ceder, capitular, entregar
    Surrender: Rescate, rendición
    Surrender value: Valor de rescate
Survey (to): Inspeccionar, peritar
    Survey: Inspección, peritaje
    Surveyors: Inspector, perito

T

Tackle: Aparejo
Tally: Inventario
Tank: Tanque
    Hopper tank: Tanque alimentador
Tariff: Arancel, impuesto, tarifa
Tax: Impuesto, gravamen
Tender (to): Presentarse a un concurso o licitación para obtener un contrato

Termination: Cancelación

Through transportation: Transporte directo

Through traffic: Tráfico de larga distancia

Tide: Marea

Time Bar: Plazo

Tonnage: Tonelaje

Tort (in): Extracontractual

Tow (to): Remolcar

    Towage: Remolque, derechos de remolque

    Towboat: Remolcador

    Towline: Estacha/Cuerda de remolque

    Tow-worthiness: Remolcable

Trade: Comercio

    Trading company: Compañía de comercio exterior

Tramp vessel: Buque de tráfico irregular

Tranship (to): Transbordar, transitar

    Transhipment: Transbordo, tránsito

Trapping: Captura, retención

Trimming: Trimaje, arrumaje. Nivelación de la carga para asegurar su estabilidad dentro de un buque en una travesía

Trip charter/Trip out: Modalidad del fletamento por tiempo, por periodos no especificados, sino determinados por la duración de una travesía concreta

Trustee: Fideicomisario, fiduciario

Tug: Remolcador

    Tugowner: Propietario del remolcador

U

Unberth (to): Desatracar

Undergo (to): Realizar, llevar a cabo

Underlying Registry: Registro subsidiario

Undertaking: Tarea

Underwater parts/body: Parte sumergida, obra viva del casco

Underwriter: Asegurador, empresa aseguradora

Undocking: Desatraque

Unit load: Unidad de carga

Unitization: Carga unitarizada para facilitar su manipulación

V

Venture: Empresa, tarea emprendida
Vessel: Buque
    Carrying vessel: Buque con derecho de paso
    Non-carrying vessel: Buque sin derecho de paso
    Salving vessel: Buque de salvamento
    Vessel's Yard Building: Astillero
Victual (to): Abastecer, avituallar
Void: Nulo, inválido
Voyage: Travesía
    Scrap voyage: Ultima travesía de un buque

W

Waiver: Exención, exoneración
Watch: Guardia
Warehouse (to): Almacenar
    Warehouse: Almacén
    Warehousing: Almacenaje
Warrant (to): Garantizar, asegurar
    Warrant/Warranty: Garantía, póliza
    Warranty: Titular de una garantía
Wastage: Desgaste, desperdicio
Waterway: Vía navegable
    Inland waterways: Vías navegables interiores
Waybill: Hoja de ruta
Wear and tear: Desgaste, deterioro por uso
Weight: Peso
Wharf: Dársena, muelle
Wholesale: Venta al por mayor
Willful: Intencionado, premeditado
Winch: Cabestrante, torno para elevar pesos
    Winchman: Maquinillero, operario encargado del torno
Winding up: Liquidación
Withdrawal: Retirada

Withhold (to): Denegar, rehusar
Working days: Días laborables
Workmanship: Hechura, acabado
Wreck: Naufragio, restos de un naufragio

9
Glosario de transporte marítimo

1. Español-Inglés

A

A bordo: Aboard, on board, shipboard
A flote: Afloat
A granel: In bulk
A la deriva: Adrift
A tanto alzado: Lump sum
Abastecimiento: Supply
Abordaje: Boarding
Acuerdo: Agreemente, settlement
Acreedor hipotecario: Mortgagee
Acuse de recibo: Acknowledgement of receipt
Adquisición: Acquisition
Aduanas: Customs House
Agente de aduanas: Custom broker
Agente de compras: Procurement man
Agente de seguros: Insurance broker
Agente marítimo: Broker
Almacenar: To store, to warehouse
    Almacén: Store, warehouse
    Almacenamiento: Storage, warehousing
Alquiler: Hire
    Alquiler por fletamento: Charter hire
Ambito: Scope
Amante (cabo grueso): Runner
Amarrar: To moor
    Amarraje: Mooring
Aparejo: Tackle
Apresamiento: Seizure
Arancel: Tariff, duty
    Arancel de aduanas: Customs tariff
Arbitraje: Arbitration
Armador: Shipowner
    Armador disponente: Disponent shipwoner

Arrendador: Hirer
Arribada: Putting in
Arrumaje: Trimming
Asegurar: To insure
    Asegurado: Insurant, insured
    Asegurador: Insurer, underwriter
Asignar: To allocate
Astillero: Dockyard, shipyard, vesse's yard building
Atracar: To call at, to dock
    Atraque: Docking
    Atraque forzoso: Forced call
Autoridad Portuaria: Port/Harbour Authority
Aval: Bank guarantee
Avería: Average
    Avería general: General average
    Avería gruesa: General average
    Avería particular: Particular average
Aviso a los navegantes: Notice to mariners
Avituallar: To victual

B

Bajo cubierta: Under deck
Balizar: To buoy
Baliza: Beacon
    Balizaje: Beaconage, buoyage
Bancarrota: Bankruptcy
Bandera: Flag
    Bandera de conveniencia: Flag of convenience
Barcaza: Barge, lighter
Barrera: Bar
Beneficio: Profit
Bloqueo: Blockade, blockage
Bodega: Hold
Bolardo: Bollard
Boya: Buoy
Buque: Ship, vessel

Buque con derecho de paso: Carrying vessel
Buque de salvamento: Salving vessel
Buque de tráfico irregular: Tramp vessel
Buque sin derecho de paso: Non-carrying vessel

C

Cabrestrante: Winch
Calado: Draught
Caldera: Boilers
Cámara de Comercio: Chamber of Commerce
Cambio de ruta: Deviation
Cancelación: Termination
Capitán: Master. El término *Captain* es una forma coloquial, aunque no exacta, de uso entre la tripulación del buque
    Capitán de Marina Mercante: Master Mariner
Captura: Trapping
Cargar: To load
    Carga embalada: Package
    Carga suelta: Loose cargo
    Carga total: Burden
    Carga unitarizada (para facilitar su manipulación): Unitization
    Carga: Cargo, load
    Cargamento: Shipload
    Cargamento sobre cubierta: Deck load
Carta: Letter
    Carta de alistamiento: Notice of readiness
    Carta de crédito: Letter of credit
Casco: Hull
Cesionario: Assignee
    Cesión: Assignment
Chimenea: Funnel
Cierre patronal: Lockout
Cláusula: Clause
    Cláusula de cese de arrendamiento: Off hire clause
    Cláusula de arbitraje: Arbitration clause

Cláusula de avería gruesa: General Average clause
Cláusula de cambio de ruta: Deviation clause
Cláusula de colisión por culpa concurrente: Both to blame and collision clause
Cláusula de colisión: Running down clause
Cláusula de consolidación: Option to consolidate
Claúsula de desembarque: Landing clause
Cláusula de garantía: Guarantee clause
Cláusula de máxima importancia: Paramount clause
Cláusula de navegabilidad: Seaworthiness clause
Cláusula de no responsabilidad en huelgas, motines y conmociones civiles: Free of strikes, riots and civil commotions clause
Cláusula de pérdida total virtual: Constructive total loss clause
Cláusula de prontitud razonable: Reasonable dispatch clause
Cláusula de prórroga de cobertura: Continuation clause
Cláusula de rescisión: Cancellation/contestable clause
Cláusula de riesgo de apresamiento excluido: Free of capture and seizure clause
Cláusula de sustitución: Superseding clause
Cláusula depósito a depósito: Warehouse to warehouse clause
Cláusula en la que se establece el derecho de retención sobre las mercancías: Lien clause
Cláusula en la que se establece la cesión de responsabilidad: Cesser clause
Cláusula excluyente de responsabilidad del asegurador sobre los bienes bajo custodia del asegurado: Care, custody or control exclusion clause
Cláusula para seguros de carga: Institute cargo clause
Cláusula por la que se reembolsa al asegurado los gastos incurridos en caso de siniestro: Sue and labour clause
Cláusula restrictiva de responsabilidad del transportista: New Jason clause
Cláusulas particulares adicionales: Riders
Cobrar: To charge
Comerciante: Merchant
Comercio: Trade
Comisión de corretaje: Brokerage commission
Compensación: Set-off
Compañía de comercio exterior: Trading company
Compañía naviera: Shipping company
Compartimentos: Appurtenances

Conocimiento de embarque: Bill of Lading
Consignatario receptor: Consignee
Consignatario emisor: Consignor
Construcción naval: Shipbuilding
Constructor naval: Shipbuilder
Contenedor: Container
Contrademanda: Counterclaim
Contrato: Agreement, contract
   Contratista: Contractor
   Contrato de alquiler: Hire agreement
   Contrato de arrendamiento: Lease contract
   Contrato de construcción: Building contract
   Contrato de salvamento: Salvage agreement
   Contrato de venta: Purchase agreement
Convenio: Agreement, settlement
Corredera: Log
Corredor marítimo: Shipbroker
Costes: Charges, costs, expenses
   Costes de salvamento: Salvage charges/expenses
Cuaderno de bitácora: Log book
Cuadrilla: Gang
Cuarentena: Quarantine
Cubertada (carga en cubierta): Deck cargo
Cubierta: Deck
Cuenta de escala: Disbursement account
Cuentas bancarias: Accounts
Cumplir con: To comply with
   Cumplimiento: Compliance
Cuño: Seal
Cuota: Dues, instalment

D

Daño: Damage
   Daños y perjuicios: Damages
Dársena: Wharf

Declaración: Notice
    Declaración de daños: Notice of claim
    Declaración de embarque: Notice of shipment
Decomiso: Seizure
Defectos ocultos: Latent defects
Demandar: To claim
    Demanda: Claim
    Demanda por daños y perjuicios: Claim damages
    Demandante: Claimant
Demora: Demurrage
Depósito: Bunker
Depositario de bienes: Bailee
Derecho marítimo: Admiralty Law
Derechos: Rights, duties
    Derechos de aduana: Customs duties
    Derechos de despacho aduanero: Customs clearance
    Derechos de franqueo: Stamp rights
    Derechos de muelle: Dockage, quayage
    Derechos especiales de giro (DEG): Special Drawing Rights (SDR)
    Derechos portuarios: Anchorage duties, port duties
Derrame: Leakage
Desatracar: To unberth
    Desatraque: Undocking
Descargar: To discharge
Desembarcar: To load (mercancías), to disembark (pasajeros)
    Desembarcadero: Jetty, landing stage
    Desembarque: Disembarkation, unloading
Desembolso: Disbursement
Desgaste: Wear and Tear
Desguazador: Shipbreaker
Despachar en aduanas: To clear customs
    Despachante de aduanas: Customs dealer/clearer
    Despacho aduanero: Clearance for customs
Despacho del buque (autorización sanitaria previa a la entrada/salida en puerto): Ship's clearance

Desperdicio: Wastage
Destinatario: Receiver
Devengar: To accrue
Devolución: Redelivery
Días laborables/hábiles: Working days, banking days
Días naturales: Running days, calendar days
Dique seco: Drydock
Disposición: Disposal
Divisa: Currency
Documento de embarque: Shipping document
Documento de embarque marítimo: Sea waybill

E

Echazón: Jettison
Ejecutar: To perform
   Ejecución: Performance
Eliminar: To delete
   Eliminación: Deletion
Embalaje: Packing
Embarcar: To ship, to board
   Embarque: Shipment
   Embarcación: Craft
Embargo: Levy, seizure
   Embargo naval, hipoteca naval: Lien on a vessel
   Embargo preventivo: Lien
Emitir: To issue
   Emisión: Issue
   Emisor: Issuer
Empleado: Servant
En cubierta: On deck
En efectivo: Cash
En nombre de: On behalf of
En peligro: In distress
En tierra: Ashore
En virtud de: Pursuant to

Encallar: To strand
Endosar: To endorse
    Endoso: Endorsement
Engranaje: Gear
Enmienda: Amendment
Entrega: Delivery
    Entrega al costado del buque: Overside delivery
    Entrega contra aceptación: Delivery against acceptance
    Entrega contra pago: Delivery against payment
    Entrega errónea: Misdelivery
Envío: Consignment
Equipamiento: Outfit
Eslinga: Sling
Estacha (cuerda de remolque): Towline
Etiqueta roja (para mercancías peligrosas): Red label
Escala: Stoppage
Escotilla: Hatch
Escritura de compraventa: Bill of Sale
Escritura de convenio: Deed of convenant
Estibar: To stevedore, to stow
    Estiba: Stevedoring, stowage
    Estibador: Longshoreman, stevedore
Estipulación: Provision
Evacuar: To evacuate
    Evacuación: Evacuation
Exención: Waiver
Expedición (mercancías): Dispatch, sending, shipping
Exportación: Export
Extracontractual: In tort

F

Factura: Invoice
Falso flete: Deadfreight
Fardo: Bale
Faro: Lighthouse

Fecha de entrega: Delivery date
Fecha de vencimiento: Closing date
Fianza: Bail
Fideicomisario: Trustee
Firma: Signature
Fletar: To chart
   Fletador: Charterer, shipper
   Fletamento: Affreightment, charter
   Fletamento por tiempo no determinado: Round trip
   Flete: Freight
   Flete de regreso: Backfreight
   Flete pagadero en destino: Freight collect, freight payable on delivery
   Flete total: Full freight
Fondear: To anchor, to berth
   Fondeadero: Anchorage, berth
Francobordo de verano: Summer freeboard
Franquicia: Franchise
Fuerza mayor: Act of God
Fuerza motriz: Motive power

G

Gabarra: Barge
Garantía bancaria: Letter of indemnity
Garantizar: To warrant
   Garantía: Warrant
Gastos: Charges, expenses, expenditure
   Gastos de transporte: Carriage charges
   Gastos en destino: Charges at destination
   Gastos en origen: Charges at origin
   Gastos pagaderos en destino, paga el consignatario: Collect charges
   Gastos por empaque: Packing charges
   Gastos prepagos: Prepaid charges
   Gastos originados por la explotación comercial de un buque: Running costs
Gravamen: Encumbrance, tax
Gravar: To levy
Grúa: Crane

Grúa de brazo móvil: Derrick
Gruísta: Craneman
Guardacostas: Coast guard

H

Herramientas: Appliances
Hipotecar: To mortgage
    Hipoteca: Mortgage
    Hipoteca naval: Lien on a vessel
Hoja de ruta: Waybill
Huelga: Strike
Hundir: To sink
Hundir intencionadamente: To scuttle

I

Importación: Import
Impuesto: Tax
In bond: En depósito aduanero
Incumplimiento/ infracción: Breach
Indemnización: Compensation
Inhabilitación: Disqualification, barring
    Inhabilitado: Debarred
Innavegable: Unseaworthiness
Instalaciones: Facilities, premises
Intermediario: Middleman
Inventario: Tally

L

Lanchaje: Boatage, lighterage
Lastre: Ballast
Legal: Lawful
Ley de Transporte Marítimo de Mercancías: Carriage of Goods by Sea Act
Libre a bordo: Clean on board
Libre de derechos de aduana: Duty free
Libre plática: Free pratique

Licitar: To tender
Línea de carga de verano: Summer load line
Línea de pleamar: Shoreline
Liquidación: Winding up
Litigio: Suit at law
Llegada: Arrival

M

Manejar: To handle
   Manejo: Handling
Manga: Beam, breadth
Manifiesto de carga: Cargo manifest, entry manifest
Mantenimiento: Maintenance
Maquinillero: Winchman
Mar: Sea
   Mar en calma: Smooth waters
Marea: Tide
Marino: Mariner
Materia prima: Raw material
Medida: Measurement
Mercancía: Cargo, commodity, goods, merchandise
   Mercancía cargada por volumen: Measurement cargo/goods
   Mercancía detallada: Particulars
   Mercancías autorizadas: Lawful goods
   Mercancías defectuosas: Unsound goods
   Mercancías en depósito aduanero: Bonded goods
Motín: Mutiny, riot
Muelle: Dock, pier, quay, wharf
Multa: Fine

N

Naufragio: Wreck
Navegar: To sail, to steam
   Navegable: Seaworthy
   Navegabilidad: Seaworthiness

    Navegación: Steaming
    Naviero: Shipowner
Negligencia: Negligence
Noray: Bollard
Norma: Rule
    Normativa: Regulation
Notificar (al destinatario): To notify (party)
    Notificación: Notice
    Notificación de arribo: Notice of readiness
    Notificación, aviso de cancelación: Notice of cancellation
    Notificación de daños: Notice of damage
    Notificación de reclamación: Notice of protest
Nulo: Void
Nulo y sin efecto: Null and void
Nudo: Knot

O

Obligado a: Bound to
Obligatorio: Compulsory
Obra viva del casco: Underwater parts/body
Obstaculizar: To hinder
    Obstáculo: Hazard, hindrance
Oficial: Mate
Orden de entrega: Delivery order
Orilla: Shore

P

Pagar los derechos de aduana: To custom
Pagaré: Bond
Paleta: Pallet
Pañol: Store
Paquete: Parcel
Pérdida: Loss
    Pérdida efectiva total: Actual total loss
    Pérdida efectiva virtual: Constructive total loss
Perecedero: Perishable

Periodo de fletamento: Charter period
Periodo de gracia: Grace period
Peritaje: Joint survey
Permiso de embarque: Broker's order
Peso: Weight
    Peso bruto: Gross weight
    Peso efectivo: Outturn weight
    Peso neto: Net weight
Pie: Foot
    Pies: Feet
Piezas de repuesto: Spare parts
Pillaje: Pilferage
Piratería: Piracy
Plano de Estiba: Stowage plan
Plazo: Time bar
Poder notarial: Letter of attorney, letter of delegation
Póliza: Policy
    Póliza de seguro: Insurance policy
    Póliza de seguro total: Endowment policy
    Póliza de fletamento: Charter Party
Popa: Aft
Práctico: Pilot
    Practicaje: Pilotage
Precinto: Seal
Precio: Price
    Precio de mercado: Current market price
Premeditado: Willful
Prestamista: Lender
Previsión: Forecast
Prima: Premium
    Prima por el salvamento: Salvage award
Privación: Deprivation
Proa: Fore
Procedimientos: Proceedings
Producto: Commodity
Profundidad: Depth

Promulgar: To enact
    Promulgación: Enactment
Propiedad: Property
Propietario: Owner
    Propietario de un buque: Shipowner
Prórroga: Renewal
Proveer: To supply
    Proveedor: Supplier, chandler
Pulgada: Inch
Puerto: Port, harbour
    Puerto de aprovisionamiento de combustible: Bunkering port
    Puerto de carga: Port of loading
    Puerto de descarga: Port of discharge/port of delivery
    Puerto de escala: Port of call
    Puerto de refugio, de recalada forzosa: Port of distress
    Puerto franco: Free port

R

Recalada: Putting back
Receptor: Receiver
Recibo: Receipt
    Recibo del piloto: Mate's receipt
Recompensa: Reward
    Recompensa por el salvamento: Salvage reward
Recuperar: To repossess
Reembarcar: To reship
    Reembarque: Reshipment
Reembolsar: To reimburse
    Reembolso: Reimbursement
Referencia: Mark
Registro: Registry
    Registro subsidiario: Underlying registry
Reglamento: Regulation
Remesa: Remittance
Remolcar: To tow

Remolcable: Tow-worthiness
Remolcador: Towboat, tugboat
Remolque: Towage
Rendición: Surrender
Rendimiento neto: Outturn
Responsabilidad civil: Liability
Restricciones laborales: Restraints of labour
Retirada: Withdrawal
Retrasar: To delay
Retraso: Delay
Riesgo: Risk, hazard
Rompeolas: Breakwater
Ruta: Route
Rutas convencionales: Customary routes

S

Salida: Departure
Salvar: To save
Salvador (persona o buque): Salvor
Salvamento: Salvage
Sanción: Penalty
Seguro: Insurance
Sin llegada, no hay venta: No arrival, no sale
Sin salvamento, no hay pago: No cure, no pay
Sobrestadía: Demurrage
Sociedad de Clasificación: Classification Society
Solicitud: Requisition
Soltar amarras: To cast off
Subarriendo: Subset
Subflete: Sub-freight
Suministro de combustible: Bunkering

T

Tanque: Tanque
Tanque alimentador: Hopper tank

Tarea: Undertaking
Tarifa: Rate, tariff
   Tarifa de fletamento: Charter rate
   Tarifa de flete: Freight rate
Tasar: To assess
   Tasación: Assessment
   Tasa: Fee
Temerariamente: Recklessly
Tiempo de plancha: Laytime, laydays
Timonel: Steersman
Titular: Holder
Tonelaje: Tonnage
   Tonelaje de desplazamiento: Displacement tonnage
   Tonelaje de peso muerto: Deadweight tonnage
Tráfico de larga distancia: Through traffic
Tráfico marítimo de corta distancia: Short Sea Shipping
Trámites: Proceedings
Transbordar: To tranship
   Transbordo: Transhipment
Tránsito: Transhipment
Transitario: Forwarder, forwarding agent
Transporte: Transport, conveyance
   Transporte directo: Through transportation
   Transportista: Carrier
   Transportista independiente: Outsider
Travesía: Voyage
   Travesía en lastre: Ballast voyage
   Travesía última de un buque: Scrap voyage
Trimaje: Trimming
Trincar: To lash
Tripular: To man
   Tripulación: Crew

U

Unidad de carga: Unit load

V

Vencimiento: Maturity
Venta al por mayor: Wholesale
Venta al por menor: Retail
Vía navegable: Waterway
    Vía navegable interior: Inland waterway
Viaje: Journey, voyage
Víctimas: Casualties

10
Siglas del transporte marítimo

A

AAR *Against all risks*
Contra todo riesgo.

A.F. *Advanced Freight*
Flete adelantado.

B

BAF *Bunker Adjustment Factor*
Factor de ajuste por combustible.

BDI *Both dates included*
Ambas fechas incluidas.

BIMCO *Baltic and International Maritime Council*
Consejo Marítimo Báltico e Internacional.

B/L: *Bill of Lading*
Conocimiento de embarque.

B.S. *Bunker Surcharge*
Sobrecarga por combustible.

C

CAD *Cash against documents*
Pago contra documentos.

CAF *Currency Adjustment Factor*
Factor de ajuste por el cambio monetario.

CBD *Cash before delivery*
Pago antes de la entrega de la mercancía.

CFL *Cost, freight, landed*
Coste, flete y descarga.

CFS *Container Freight Station*
Área en la que se recibe la carga general, para ser cargada en contenedores consolidados.

C/L *Container Load*
Carga del contenedor.

CP *Charter Party*
Contrato de fletamento.

COB *Cargo on Board*
Mercancía a bordo.

COD *Cash on Delivery*
Entrega contra reembolso.

COS *Cash on Shipment*
Pago contra embarque.

CSC *Container Service Charges*
Cargas por servicios a contenedores.

CSP *Container Service Port*
Puerto de servicios a contenedores.

CST *Container Service Tariff*
Tarifa por servicios a contenedores.

COW *Crude Oil Washing*
Sistema de limpieza de los tanques de carga de fuel.

D

d/a *Delivery against acceptance*
Entrega contra aceptación.

d.f. *Dead Freight*
Falso flete.

D/A *Disbursement Account*
Cuenta de escala.

DF *Documentation Fee*
Tasas por documentación.

D&H *Dangerous and hazardous cargo*
Mercancía peligrosa.

D.O. *Delivered Order*
Nota de entrega.

D/P *Delivered against Payment*
Entrega de documentos contra pago.

DUVEV *Unified Document of dispatch of vessel*
DUE Documento Unico de Escala.

DW *Dead weight*
Peso muerto.

DWT *Deadweight Tonnage*
Tonelaje de peso muerto (TPM).

E

EDI *Electronic Data Interchange*
Intercambio Electrónico de datos.

EEZ *Exclusive Economic Zone*
Zona Económica Exclusiva.

E&OE *Error and Omission Excepted*
Salvo error y omisión.

ELS *Extra Length Surcharge*
Recargo de bultos extralargos.

ETA *Estimated Time of Arrival*
Tiempo estimado de llegada.

ETD *Estimated Time of Departure*
Tiempo estimado de salida.

EWS *Extra Weight Surcharge*
Recargo por bultos pesados.

F

FAK *Freight all kinds*
Tarifa estándar, independientemente de las mercancías transportadas en un contenedor.

FEU *Forty Feet Equivalent Unit*
Medida equivalente a 40 pies.

FC&S *Free from General Average*
Libre de avería particular (LAP).

FC&S *Free of Capture and Seizure*
Riesgo de apresamiento excluido.

FCL *Full Container Load*
Contenedor completo.

FGA *Free of General Average*
Libre de avería gruesa.

FILO *Free in Liner Out (V. LIFO)*
(Sin gastos de carga, sí de descarga).

FLO/FLO *Float-on/Float-off*
Transflotación.

FOC *Flag of convenience*
Bandera de conveniencia.

G

g.a. *General Average*
Avería general.

GATT *General Agreement on Tariffs and Trade*
Acuerdo General sobre Aranceles Aduaneros y Comercio.

GDP *Gross Domestic Product*
Producto Interior Bruto.

GNP *Gross National Product*
Producto Nacional Bruto.

GMDSS *Global Maritime Distress and Safety System*
Sistema Marítimo Internacional de Emergencia y Seguridad.

Gr.Wt *Gross Weight*
Peso bruto.

GT *Gross Tonnage*
Tonelaje bruto.

I

ICS *International Chamber of Shipping*
Cámara Naviera Internacional.

IMCO *Inter-governmental Maritime Consultive Organisation*
Organización Intergubernamental Marítima de Consulta.

IMDG *International Maritime Dangerous Goods Code*
Código Marítimo Internacional para mercancías peligrosas.

IMO *International Maritime Organisation*
Organización Marítima Internacional (OMI).

ISO *International Organization for Standarisation*
Organización Internacional de Normalización.

IOU *I owe you*
Pagaré.

J

JIT *Just in Time*
Justo a tiempo.

L

L/C *Letter of Credit*
Carta de credito.

LCM *Lateral Cargo Mobility*
Movilidad de carga lateral.

L/D *Loading/Discharging*
Carga/Descarga.

LIFO *Liner In Free Out* (V. FILO)
(sí gastos de carga, no de descarga).

LMAA *London Maritime Arbitrators Association*
Asociación de Arbitraje Marítimo de Londres.

LNG *Carrier Liquefied Natural Gas Carrier*
Carguero de gas natural licuado.

LOA *Length over all*
Eslora total o máxima.

LPG Carrier *Liquefied Petroleum Gas Carrier*
Carguero de gas de petróleo licuado.

M

MABL *Master Bill of Lading*
Conocimiento de embarque principal.

MR *Mate's Receipt*
Recibo del piloto.

MRCC *Maritime Rescue Co-ordination Centre*
Centro Marítimo de Coordinación de Operaciones de Rescate.

m/s *Months sight*
A meses vista.

MSC *Maritime Safety Committee*
Comité de Seguridad Marítimo.

MV *Motor vessel*
Buque, nave.

N

NT *Net Tonnage*
Tonelaje neto.

NUC *Not Under Command.*
Sin control. Fuera de control.

O

OBO Ship *Ore/Bulk/Oil Ship*
Carguero de mineral, granel y combustible.

O/D *Over Deck*
Sobre Cubierta.

P

p.a. *Per annum*
Anual.

P&I *Protection and Indemnity Club*
Club de Protección e Indemnización.

POD *Proof of Delivery*
Prueba de entrega.

POD *Pay on Delivery*
Pago contra entrega.

POE *Port of Entry*
Puerto de entrada.

POL *Petroleum, oil and lubricants*
Crudos, petróleo y lubricantes.

S

SDR *Special Drawing Rights*
Derechos Especiales de Giro (DEG).

SOLAS *Safety of Life at Sea Convention*
Convención para la seguridad de la vida humana en el mar.

SR&CC *Strike, Riots and Civil Commotions*
Huelga, alzamientos y conmociones civiles.

SSH *Saturday, Sunday, Holiday*
Sábados, domingos y festivos.

STC *Said to contain*
Dice contener. Expresión utilizada para referirse al contenido de un embalaje cerrado.

STW *Said to weight*
Dice pesar. Expresión utilizada para referirse al contenido de un embalaje cerrado.

T

TEU *Twenty Feet Equivalent Unit*
Medida equivalente a 20 pies, utilizada para indicar la capacidad de los buques.

THC *Terminal Handling Charge*
Cantidad fija que los explotadores del buque han de abonar en concepto de manipulación de mercancía en puerto. Esta cantidad varía según cada puerto.

T/S *Transhipment*
Transbordo.

U

ULCC *Ultra Large Crude Carrier*
Tanquero de gran capacidad (Más de 300.000 tpm).

ULD *Unitary Load Device*
Dispositivo unitario de carga.

V

VLCC *Very Large Crude Carrier*
Tanquero de gran capacidad (Entre 200.000 – 300.000 tpm).

VTS *Vessel Traffic Service*
Servicios diseñados para mejorar la seguridad y la eficiencia del tráfico marítimo y proteger el entorno.

W

WA *With average*
Con avería.

WOR *Without our responsability*
Sin responsibilidad por nuestra parte.

WPA *With particular average*
Con avería particular.

WRS *War Risk Surcharge*
Recargo por riesgo de guerra.

WWD *Weather Working Days*
Días en los que la climatología permite trabajar.

Bibliografía

- Alas, C. *Diccionario Jurídico-Comercial del Transporte Marítimo.* Universidad de Oviedo, Oviedo, 1983.
- Aranzábal, F. J. *Manual Práctico de Inglés Marítimo.* Colección Itxaso. Departamento de Agricultura y Pesca del Gobierno Vasco. Vitoria, 1995.
- Branch, A. E. *Dictionary of Shipping International Business Trade Terms and Abbreviations.* Ed. Witherby & Co. London, 1995.
- Buelga, J. & Wilson, D. *English for Maritime Commerce.* Colegio de Oficiales de la Marina Mercante. Iberediciones, S. L. Madrid, 1994.
- Coto Millán, P. *Maritime Transport Applied Economics.* Ed. Civitas. Madrid, 1999.
- Chevalier, D. & Duphil, E. *Le Transport.* Éditions Foucher. París, 2000.
- Freire Seoane, Mª J. & González Laxe, F. *Economía del Transporte Marítimo.* Ed. Netbiblo. A Coruña, 2003.
- González Lebrero, R.A. *Curso de Derecho de la Navegación.* Servicio Central de Publicaciones del Gobierno Vasco. Vitoria-Gasteiz, 1998.
- *IMO Standard Marine Communication Phrases.* International Maritime Organization, London, 2002.
- *Incoterms 1990.* Cámara de Comercio Internacional. Barcelona, 1990.
- León, A. & Romero, R. *Logística del Transporte Marítimo.* Logis Book. Barcelona, 2003.
- López, E.; Spiegelberg, J.M. & Carrillo, F. *Inglés Técnico Naval.* Servicio de publicaciones de la Universidad de Cádiz. Cádiz, 1991.
- Luddeke, C. and Contributors. *Marine Claims. A guide for the handling and prevention of marine claims.* LLP Limited. London, 1996.
- *Marpol 73/78* International Maritime Organisation. London, 2002.
- Palacio López, P. *Transporte Marítimo de Contenedores: Organización y Gestión.* Fundación Instituto Portuario de Estudios y Cooperación de la Comunidad Valenciana. Valencia, 2001.
- Pulido Begines, J. L. *Los contratos de remolque marítimo.* J. M. Bosch Editor. Barcelona, 1996.
- Romero, R. *El Transporte Marítimo. Introducción a la Gestión del Transporte Marítimo.* Logis Book. Barcelona, 2002.
- Stopford, M. *Maritime Economics.* Ed. Routledge. London, 1997.

PÁGINAS WEB CONSULTADAS

- BIMCO

http://www.bimco.dk

- DERECHO MARITIMO

http://www.derechomaritimo.info

- ERASMUS UNIVERSITEIT ROTTERDAM

http://web.eur.nl/

- ESCUELA SUPERIOR DE LA MARINA CIVIL. GIJON

http://web.uniovi.es/marina/utils/utilidades.htm

- INSTITUTO UNIVERSITARIO DE ESTUDIOS MARÍTIMOS

http://www.udc.es/iuem

- PLOIKI MARITIME & TRADING, S.A.

http://www.ploiki.gr/academic.html

- THE TRANSPORTATION INSTITUTE

http://www.trans-inst.org/seawords.htm

- THE INTERNATIONAL MARITIME ORGANIZATION

http://www.imo.org

- UNCTAD. UNITED NATIONS FOR TRADE AND DEVELOPMENT

http://www.unctad.org

- MALMÖ UNIVERSITY

http://www.mah.se

Las señales marítimas internacionales de banderas

International Maritime Signal Flags

ALPHABET-ALFABETO

I have a diver down; keep clear at slow speed.	*I am taking in, discharging or carrying dangerous cargo.*	*"Yes" or "Affirmative".*

A-ALPHA	B-BRAVO	C-CHARLIE
Buzo sumergido. Manténgase alejado de mí y a poca velocidad.	Estoy cargando, descargando o transportando mercancías peligrosas.	Afirmativo "SI."

I am maneuvering with difficulty. Keep clear.	*I am directing my course to starboard.*	*I am disabled, communicate with me.*

D-DELTA	E-ECHO	F-FOXTROT
Estoy maniobrando con dificultad, manténgase alejado de mí.	Caigo a estribor.	Tengo avería, póngase en comunicación conmigo.

I require a pilot.	*I have a pilot on board.*	*I am directing my course to port.*

G - GOLF	H - HOTEL	I - INDIA
Necesito práctico.	Tengo práctico a bordo.	Caigo a babor.

I am on fire and have dangerous cargo; keep clear.	*I wish to communicate with you.*	*You should stop your vessel immediately.*

J-JULIET	K-KILO	L-LIMA
Incendio a bordo, manténgase alejado.	Deseo comunicar con usted", o "invitación para transmitir".	Pare su buque inmediatamente.

My vessel is stopped; making no way.	*"No" or "Negative".*	*Man overboard.*

M-MIKE	N-NOVEMBER	O-OSCAR
Mi buque está parado y sin arrancada.	Negativo "NO".	¡Hombre al agua!

*All personnel return to ship; proceeding to sea (**in port**). At sea, it may be used by fishing vessels to mean, "My nets have come fast upon an obstruction".*	*Ship meets health regulations; request clearance into port.*	*None.*

P-PAPA	Q-QUEBEC	R-ROMEO
En puerto. Todo el personal debe regresar a bordo por tener el buque que hacerse a la mar. **En el mar**. Puede ser usada por barcos pesqueros para significar: "mis redes se han enganchado".	Mi buque cumple los requisitos sanitarios; pido libre plática.	Nada.

Inglés marítimo

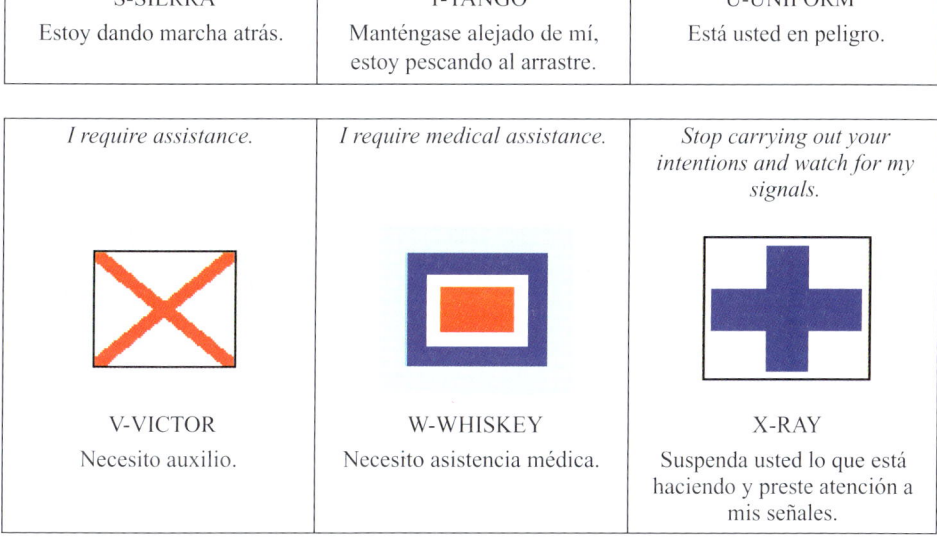

REPEATERS-SEÑALES DE REPETICIÓN

Repeat First Flag.		Repita la Primera Bandera.
Repeat Second Flag.		Repita la Segunda Bandera.
Repeat Third Flag.		Repita la Tercera Bandera.

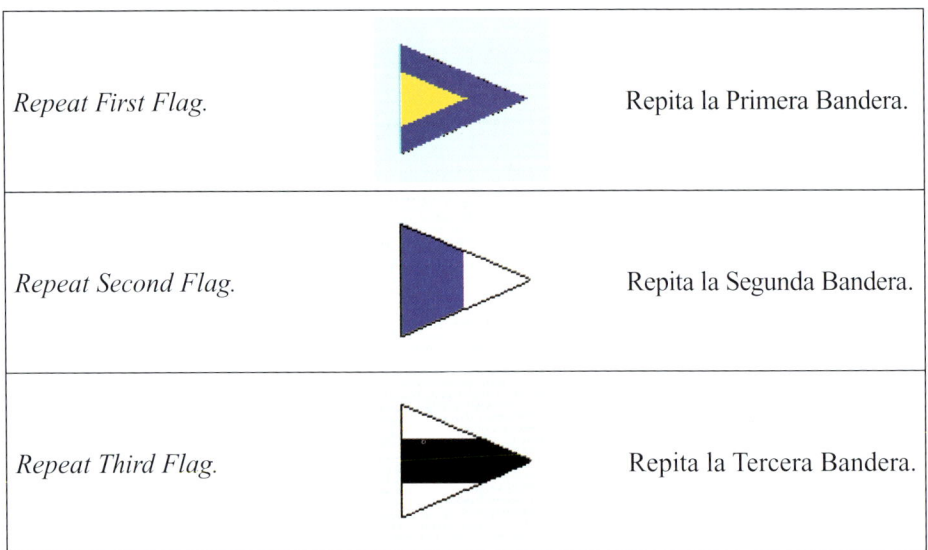

NUMERALS-NÚMEROS

Zero.		Cero.
One.		Uno.
Two.		Dos.
Three.		Tres.
Four.		Cuatro.
Five.		Cinco.
Six.		Seis.
Seven.		Siete.
Eight.		Ocho.
Nine.		Nueve.
End of Message.		Fin del Mensaje.

Galería de imágenes

Crude carrier-Petrolero.

Icebraker-Rompehielos.

Fishing Vessel-Barco pesquero.

Cruiser-Crucero.

Ro-ro Carrier-Carguero Ro-ro.

Tug boat-Remolcador.

Salvage Vessel-Buque de salvamento.

Unload-Descarga.

Stowage-Estiba.

Berth-Atraque.

Handling Cargo-Manejo de la carga.

All Weather Terminal-Terminal cubierta.

Container Terminal-Terminal de contenedores.

Coal Terminal-Terminal de carbón.

Quayside Crane-Grúa de muelle.

Quayside Crane-Grúa de muelle.

Frame Crane/Gantry Crane/ Portal Crane-Grúa Pórtico.

Deck Crane- Grúa de cubierta.

Jenny Winch-Grúa de brazo rígido.

Floating Crane-Grúa Flotante.